The Formulation of AIDS Policies: Legal Considerations for Schools

Matthew J. Welker and Sarah W. J. Pell

No. 44 in the NOLPE Monograph/Book Series

DISCLAIMER

The National Organization on Legal Problems of Education (NOLPE) is a nonadvocacy association of educators and attorneys. The views expressed in this publication are those of the authors and do not represent official views of the organization.

ABOUT THE AUTHORS

MATTHEW WELKER received his Associate of Arts degree from Miami Dade Community College, Miami, Florida. He received his Bachelor of Science degree in chemistry, a Bachelor of Science education and his Doctor of Science degree in administration and supervision from Florida International University — the University of Florida at Miami. He has worked as a science teacher, department chairperson and resident teacher in Dade County Public Schools' Dade Academy for the Teaching Arts. He is currently an assistant principal at Carol City Senior High School in Miami.

SARAH PELL received her Bachelors, Masters and Doctorate from Duke University in Durham, North Carolina. She has worked as a teacher in both elementary and secondary schools, as a Superintendent of Public Instruction in Kodiak, Alaska, and professor in education at St. Andrew's Presbyterial College in Laurenberg, North Carolina. For the past twenty years, she has been a professor of administration, supervision and school law at Florida International University — the University of Florida at Miami.

TABLE OF CONTENTS

LIST OF FIGURES AND TABLES

FIGURES

TABLES

CHAPTER I
INTRODUCTION - AIDS, THE "NEW DISEASE"

Background

Since its identification in 1981, the disease now recognized as acquired immunodeficiency syndrome or AIDS has grown from an obscure medical anomaly to become one of the world's greatest health threats. Efforts to control this biological conundrum have been complicated by the presence of complex legal, scientific and social problems that have thrust the educational community into the center of a controversy involving public and private rights. Educators quickly found that they had neither the expertise nor the experience to cope effectively with a problem of this. Educators need a policy paradigm, benchmarks and guidance, that facilitate establishment of a socially responsible and legally defensible policy response to the dilemma of AIDS within the public school environment.

Human existence on this planet has been punctuated by catastrophic epidemic events that have claimed the lives of millions of inhabitants throughout history. Probably the most significant of these events was the pandemic of bubonic plague, or Black Death, which occurred during the thirteenth and fourteenth centuries. During its 150-year rampage, the bubonic plague claimed more than 25 million human lives throughout the continents of Europe and Asia.[1] Concurrent epidemic episodes of other infectious diseases, such as typhus and syphilis, contributed significantly to the morality and social destruction that occurred during that period of history.

The pandemic of bubonic plague that decimated much of Europe also gave rise to the modern equivalent of Boards of Health and the establishment of local health departments by Italian city-states.[2] Although originally designed for surveillance purposes, the authority of local health departments was augmented considerably by outbreaks of syphilis that occurred sporadically throughout Italy during the 1600's. The prevalence of epidemic disease required the use of extraordinary health measures, such as exclusion and quarantine. At the time, these measures represented the only methods available to public health officials to control epidemic disease. Unfortunately, the social cost associated with many early health measures was exorbitant in light of their limited success in controlling epidemic

---

1. Langer, *The Black Death*, 210 SCI. 114 (1964).
2. Yankauer, *AIDS and Public Health*, 78 AMER. J. PUB. HEALTH 364 (1988).

disease. Yet, in spite of this, many of these draconian measures still remain within the arsenals of modern public health practice.

The threat of epidemic disease has waned significantly since the seventeenth century as a result of advancements in science and medicine. However in 1918, an epidemic of influenza caught the world community by surprise. Despite massive public health measures to control the disease, it spread quickly throughout the world. By the time the pandemic had subsided in 1919, the world population was reduced by more than 30 million inhabitants.[3] More recently epidemics of rabies, cholera, measles, and malaria are occurring with increasing frequency throughout the world.[4] Each day, medical researchers are confronted by new strains of microorganisms that could potentially change the course of human existence.

During the summer of 1981, a few alert physicians in New York and California reported an unusual occurrence of a rare opportunistic infection known as pneumocystis carinii among a small group of previously healthy homosexual men.[5] Doctors were familiar with this disease, but the affliction had occurred previously only among elderly and severely immunosuppressed individuals. Subsequently, an unusual form of cancer known as Kaposi's sarcoma was also reported among previously healthy homosexual men. Prior to this discovery, the Kaposi's sarcoma was observed primarily in elderly men from countries surrounding the Mediterranean Sea.[6] The appearance of these two medical anomalies prompted an extensive medical and scientific investigation which resulted in the identification of a new clinical disease referred to as acquired immunodeficiency syndrome or AIDS.

Since its identification in 1981, AIDS has become the greatest threat to public health of any communicable disease within modern times. Controlling the spread of AIDS is now considered a critical priority by public health officials within the federal government.[7] Efforts to curtail the future progress of AIDS, however, are encumbered by a unique set of biological and social factors. First, the underlying disease that is associated with AIDS is currently without prevention or treatment. Second, the virus that

---

3. Swenson, *Plagues, History and AIDS*, 57 AM. SCHOLAR 183 (1988) and *see also* Perisco, *The Great Swine Flu Epidemic of 1918*, 27 AM. HERITAGE 28 (1976).
4. *Immunization Levels Inch Up, But "Conquered Diseases" Remain a Threat*, MED. WORLD NEWS 86 (1975).
5. Centers for Disease Control, *Kaposi's Sarcoma and Pneumocystis Pneumonia Among Homosexual Men - New York City and California* 30 MORBIDITY AND MORTALITY WEEKLY REPORT 305 (1981).
6. *Id.*
7. Heckler, *The Challenge of Acquired Immunodeficiency Syndrome* 103 ANNALS OF INT. MED. 655 (1985).

is responsible for the clinical development of AIDS is noted for its genetic and phenotypic variability, making development of vaccines or treatment exceedingly arduous. Third, the human immunodeficiency virus (HIV) that is associated with AIDS does not exhibit a finite incubation period, so carriers of the virus are presumed to be chronically contagious. Fourth, the major risk groups that have been associated with AIDS are vulnerable to extensive social prejudice and private discrimination, which poses special problems for public health officials seeking to identify carriers of the disease.[8]

Public health officials project that if AIDS maintains its present rate of growth, more than 360,000 people within the United States alone will develop AIDS by 1992.[9] By January, 1991, more than 161,000 cases of AIDS had been reported to the Centers for Disease Control in Atlanta, during the reporting period of 1981-1991. Of that number nearly sixty percent of these individuals had succumbed to the ravages of this fatal disease.[10]

AIDS is currently the **only** major disease in the United States where mortality is substantially increasing. The present epidemiological data on AIDS indicate that the disease has grown inexorably from relative obscurity to epidemic proportions within the United States since 1981.[11] The impact on mortality for men between 25 and 44 years of age, for minorities, and for selected cities is much higher than the national average. When the impact of this disease is considered in terms of years of potential life lost before the age of 65, AIDS increased in rank among diseases from thirteenth in 1984 to eighth in 1986, a change that reflects the young age of those it kills and the increasing number of deaths.[12]

As with other epidemic diseases in the past, the mortality and morbidity associated with AIDS have generated considerable fear and misconception within the general population regarding the disease and its potential impact on the health and welfare of society. Nowhere else is

---

8. Gostin, *Acquired Immune Deficiency Syndrome: A Review of Science, Health Policy and Law* 3 in M.D. WITT, AIDS AND PATIENT MANAGEMENT: LEGAL, ETHICAL AND SOCIAL ISSUES (1986).

9. Centers for Disease Control, *Acquired Immunodeficiency Virus and Human Immunodeficiency Virus Infection in the United States* 38 MORBIDITY AND MORTALITY WEEKLY REPORT (No. S-4, 1988), *see generally*, Morgan and Curran, *Acquired Immunodeficiency Syndrome: Current and Future Trends*, 101 PUB. HEALTH REP. 459 (1986).

10. Centers for Disease Control, *AIDS Weekly Surveillance Report - United States*, 40 MORBIDITY AND MORTALITY REPORT 1 (January 15, 1991).

11. Centers for Disease Control, *The Extent of AIDS and Indicators of Adolescent Risk*, 37 MORBIDITY AND MORTALITY REPORT 10 (No. S-2, 1988).

12. Centers for Disease Control, *Quarterly Report to the Domestic Policy Council on the Prevalence and Rate of Spread of HIV and AIDS in the United States*, 37 MORBIDITY AND MORTALITY REPORT 223 (1988).

the problem of AIDS more compelling than in this nation's public schools. On any single day, large numbers of students and teachers interact within the confines of a relative small space. The proximity of participants in this circumstance identifies the school setting as a potential site for AIDS transmission.

Events throughout the United States have demonstrated the volatile nature of the AIDS crisis. For example, in September, 1985, the announcement that a single child with AIDS would enroll in the public schools of New York City precipitated an angry boycott in two Queens school districts. Parents vowed to "stand in the school house door" to prevent children with AIDS from attending school.[13] On the first day of classes in New York City, an estimated 11,000 children remained at home to protest the decision to allow children with AIDS to attend school. At one school, disgruntled parents erected a sign stating "Enter At Your Own Risk" to scare people away from the school.[14] The incidents that followed indicate the problem has not decreased.

Rampant fears of parents have resulted in the exclusion of children with AIDS from public schools throughout the United States.[15] The most publicized case occurred in 1985 in Kokomo, Indiana, when Ryan White, a thirteen year old boy with AIDS, was denied access to public school. A suit was filed by his parents on his behalf in federal court against school officials, where they argued that AIDS is a handicap and that Ryan was being discriminated against solely on that basis.[16] One year later, Ryan was allowed to return to school after the parents of other school children dropped their legal opposition. Ryan was cleared for admission to school by the Howard County (Indiana) County Health Officer.[17] Ryan White has since died of AIDS.

Fear has permeated both sides of the AIDS problem. Generally, healthy people are afraid because they believe that AIDS is a highly contagious disease, and people with AIDS are afraid because they believe that society is rife with prejudice and discrimination. In addressing this dilemma, former Surgeon General C. Everett Koop stated:

> In addition to illness, disability and death, AIDS has brought fear of the unknown. . . . Fear can be useful when it helps people avoid behavior that puts them at risk for AIDS. On the

---

13. *Roots of AIDS Boycott*, N.Y. Times, Sept. 14, 1985, at B1.
14. Rohter, *11,000 Boycott Classes in AIDS Protest*, N.Y. Times, Sept. 10, 1985, at B1.
15. Tarr, *AIDS: The Legal Issues Widen*, NAT. L.J. 28 (Nov. 25, 1985).
16. White v. Western School Corp., No. IP 85-1192-C (S.D. Ind. 1985).
17. *AIDS Victim to Return to School*, USA Today, Feb. 20, 1986, at A2.

other hand, unreasonable fear can be as crippling as the disease itself.[18]

If the fear concerning AIDS is left unchecked, many of the social ties that bind the American society together as a nation will be broken making it very difficult to control the future course of the disease as well as the fate of those with the disease.

It is against this background of fear and misconception that educators find themselves caught in a vortex of emotion and fear that threatens to submerge public education in an ocean of ignorance.[19] The critical nature of this disease has prompted some states to exercise their police powers to protect the general public from individuals who are known to be afflicted.[20] The use of police power to regulate public health has serious implications for the educational community where the personal rights of students and adults are involved.

Currently, no general consensus has developed among the general populace regarding the use of police power in matters pertaining to public health. The use of police power has been described as a double-edged sword, untempered and without well defined edges.[21] To some the use of police powers means considerable help and defense against epidemic disease. To others, the power to regulate public health is viewed as a substantial threat to personal freedom.[22] The potential for legal conflict regarding AIDS in public schools is high considering the fear and hysteria that exists within society. The AIDS phenomenon poses a challenge for educational policy makers who seek to protect the right of students and adults against the compelling desire to protect society as a whole from the dire consequences of AIDS.

The process of AIDS policy formation is hampered by the presence of two critical defects in the field of education. First, the educational community has little or no experience in dealing with a major public health crisis within the educational environment. Second, no effective policy model has existed for public school officials to use in formulating an appropriate policy response to the dilemma created by AIDS within public schools. To compensate for these defects, the educational community must

---

18. Koop, *Surgeon General's Report on AIDS*, 102 PUB. HEALTH REP. 1 (1987).
19. Welker, *The Impact of AIDS Upon Public Schools: A Problem of Jurisprudence*, 32 WEST'S ED. L. REP. 603 (1986).
20. Gostin, *Traditional Public Health Strategies* 47 in AIDS AND THE LAW, A GUIDE FOR THE PUBLIC (H. L. Dalton & S. Burris eds. 1987).
21. Welker, *The Impact of AIDS Upon Public Schools: A Problem of Jurisprudence*, 33 WEST'S ED. L. REP. 603 (1986).
22. Morgenstern, *The Role of the Federal Government in Protecting Citizens from Communicable Diseases*. 47 CIN. L. REV. 537 (1978).

respond in a well organized and decisive manner. Public school official must arm themselves with the best scientific, educational and legal information available in order to address the various issues associated with AIDS.

This monograph addresses the interests of school policymakers who find themselves in need of a socially responsible, legally defensible AIDS policy. A policy paradigm is presented that assists in the formation of appropriate policies. Additionally, the policy paradigm introduced in this monograph will enable district policy officials to test the efficacy of existing educational policy concerning AIDS. The legal issues associated with the presence of AIDS within public schools are indeed compelling when viewed from the perspective of students and adults. The AIDS paradigm established in this monograph seeks to balance the interests of students and teachers in maintaining their personal freedoms against the necessity of protecting the general population from the ravages of this deadly, epidemic disease.

Significance

The AIDS policy paradigm presented in this monograph will facilitate the processes of policy formation and evaluation at the district level. Recognizing the present level of confusion regarding AIDS and its impact on the public school environment, this policy paradigm will provide an important mechanism for structuring school district responses to the dilemma of AIDS throughout the country.

This monograph contributes to the policy development literature of public school administration by filling part of the information void that exists within the field of education concerning pandemic diseases. Within the last few years, district policy response to epidemic disease has been complicated by public fear and misinformation. This circumstance has threatened to submerge the educational community in a sea of ignorance which advocating the use of irrational policy approaches in dealing with the dilemma created by the AIDS epidemic. The substantive and procedural due process direction provided by this monograph will enable district officials to effectively balance the health rights of the many against the personal rights of the few during the present health crisis.

CHAPTER II

WHAT IS AIDS - SCIENTIFIC AND EDUCATIONAL IMPLICATIONS

Acquired immunodeficiency syndrome (AIDS) is a serious condition that affects the body's ability to fight bacterial and viral infection. A diagnosis of AIDS is made when a person develops a life-threatening illness not usually found in a person with a normal ability to fight disease. The two diseases most often found in AIDS patients are a lung infection called pneumocystis carinii pneumonia and a rare form of cancer called Kaposi's sarcoma. Although some questions still remain concerning the causative agent for AIDS, researchers generally believe that AIDS is brought about by a unique retrovirus capable of altering specific cells within the immune systems of its victims. This unique retrovirus was first identified as either human T-lymphotropic virus type III (HTLV-III) or lymphadenopathy associated virus (LAV). To avoid confusion, the AIDS virus is now referred to as the human immunodeficiency virus or simply HIV.

Prior to 1980, the information concerning AIDS or the virus that caused it was almost nil. The explosive growth of AIDS within the global population triggered a massive scientific inquiry that subsequently yielded a substantial base of information concerning this disease and its impact upon society. Although the causative agent has been observed and identified[1] many of the scientific details concerning the AIDS virus and its infectious characteristics remain a mystery to this day.

When AIDS was first identified in the United States, many scientists thought they were observing an entirely new disease. The ability of this disease to decimate the immune systems of its victims was unprecedented in Western medical research findings. A longitudinal analysis of AIDS and its progress throughout the world has revealed a significant connection between AIDS and the continent of Africa[2]. Research suggests that the causative agent behind AIDS was present in Africa some ten years prior to its occurrence in this country.[3] Robert Gallo, of the National Cancer

---

1. Broder and Gallo, *A Pathogenic Retrovirus (HILV-III) Linked to AIDS*, 311 NEW ENG. J. MED. 1292 (1984).
2. Norman, *Africa and the Origin of AIDS*, 230 SCI. 1141 (1985).
3. Bygbjerg, *AIDS in a Danish Surgeon*, 1 LANCET 925 (1983) *See* Nahamias, Weiss, Yaa, Lee, Kodsi, Schanfield, Matthews, Bolognesi, Durack, Motulsky, Kanki, and Essex, *Evidence for Human Infection with an HTLV-III/LAV-like Virus in Central Africa*, 2 LANCET 1279 (1986); *see also* Saxinger, Levine, Dean, Dethe, Lange-Wantzin, Moghissi, Lauren, Hoh, Sarngadharan, and Gallo, *Evidence for Exposure to HTLV-III in Uganda in 1973*, 227 SCI. 1036 (1985).

Institute, reported in 1987 that a group of researchers had uncovered a virus closely related to the AIDS virus in African green monkeys. A number of prominent scientists, including Gallo, believe that a monkey virus[4] may have been involved in a species jump between the green monkey population and the human population inhabiting the same geographic area of Africa.[5]

Subsequently, evidence has been presented that tends to support the species-jump hypothesis. Scientists have discovered that only green monkeys were capable of harboring the AIDS virus.[6] Green monkeys are one of the few species of primates that interact closely with humans. It is quite possible that the simian virus was transmitted to humans through bites, bestiality, or shared food. Once inside the human gene pool, the virus may have undergone a series of mutations before it terminated in the fierce pathology of HTLV-III or acquired immunodeficiency syndrome observed in humans.[7] It seems probable that the virus associated with AIDS mutated to its lethal form sometime during the period between 1955 and 1965. The resultant virus remained isolated within specific geographic areas of Zaire well into the 1970's. Some researchers believe that this viral isolation ended when thousands of people participated in cultural exchanges between the French-speaking nations of Zaire and Haiti.[8]

Interest in AIDS developed because of an abnormal occurrence of Karposi sarcoma in young, white, middle-class males. Upon further investigation, it was determined that many of the patients had a history of homosexuality. Many reports considered the incidence of Kaposi's sarcoma, pneumocystis carinii pneumonia, and opportunistic infections in patients with no history of underlying immune deficiency. The existence of acquired immunodeficiency syndrome or AIDS as a clinical entity was confirmed in 1981 in a number of reports published by the Centers for Disease Control (CDC) in Atlanta.

In January of 1986, CDC estimated that between 1 and 1.5 million people in the United States may have been infected with the AIDS

---

4. Simian T-lymphotropic virus III (STLV-III).
5. Kanki, Durth, Becker, Dressman, McLane, and Essex, *Antibodies to Simian T-lymphotropic Retrovirus Type III in African Green Monkeys and Recognition of STLV-III Viral Proteins by AIDS and Related Sera*, 1 LANCET 1330 (1985).
6. Daniel, Letvin, King, Kannagi, Sehgal, Hunt, Kanki, Essex, and Desrosiers, *Isolation of T-cell Tropic HTLV-III-like Retrovirus from Macaques*, 228 SCI. 1202 (1985).
7. Seligmann and Gosnell, *New Theories About AIDS: The Detective Work Is Frustrating, But Researchers Are Learning More About the Nature of the Deadly Epidemic*, NEWSWEEK, Jan., 1984, at 50. *See also* Seligmann and Hager, *Tracing the Origin of AIDS*, NEWSWEEK, May, 1984, at 101.
8. Pape, Liautaud, Thomas, Mathurin, St. Armand, Boncy, Pean, Pamphile, Laroche, Dehovitz and Hohnson, *The Acquired Immunodeficiency Syndrome in Haiti*, 103 ANNALS INT. MED. 674 (1985).

virus.[9] *Newsweek* magazine stated that in 1991 an estimated 5 million Americans may be carrying the AIDS virus.[10] Researchers at CDC reported in January, 1991, that more than 161,000 patients throughout the United States had been identified by health officials under the current case definition for the national reporting of AIDS (See Figure 1). Of that group, 57% are known to have died of AIDS.[11]

Although the disease appears to be widespread in this country, Blanchet reported that the majority of the cases have been clustered in the metropolitan areas of New York, San Francisco, Miami, Newark, Houston and Los Angeles.[12] In an article considering the future incidence of AIDS, Barnes concluded that although the number of cases will increase in all age groups, the greatest increase will be observed in children under 13 years of age where the number of cases is expected to increase from over 300 in 1986 to more than 3,000 in 1991.[13] Other estimates regarding the occurrence of AIDS in children range to over 4,000 cases with an additional 8,000 cases of AIDS-related complex yet to be diagnosed.[14]

Acquired immunodeficiency syndrome is fundamentally a sexually transmitted disease through both homosexual and heterosexual contact.[15] The presence of AIDS has been identified within groups of intravenous drug users, Haitians, recipients of blood or blood products, infants born to mothers at risk, and sexual partners of heterosexual patients with AIDS.[16] Of the reported cases involving children in 1987, 80% were attributed to mothers infected with the AIDS virus. Twelve percent had received blood transfusions and 5% had received treatment for hemophilia while 3% were of undetermined origin.[17]

Persons who are infected with the AIDS virus may transmit the virus to other people. The symptoms associated with the infection remain elusive

---

9. Curran, Morgan, Hardy, Jaffe, Darrow, and Dowdle, *The Epidemiology of AIDS: Current Status and Future Prospect*, 229 SCI. 1352 (1985).
10. NEWSWEEK, Nov., 1986, at 30.
11. Centers for Disease Control, *AIDS Weekly Surveillance Report - United States*, 40 MORBIDITY AND MORTALITY WEEKLY REPORT 1 (1991).
12. K. D. BLANCHET, AIDS: A HEALTH CARE MANAGEMENT RESPONSE (1988)
13. Barnes, *Grim Projections for AIDS Epidemic*, 232 SCI. 1589 (1986).
14. *AIDS Cases Increasing Among Kids*, Chicago Trib., Feb. 2, 1987, at 1.
15. Guinan and Hardy, *Epidemiology of AIDS in Women of the United States*, 257 J. AM. MED. A. 2039 (1987).
16. Centers for Disease Control, *Update of Kaposi's Sarcoma and Opportunistic Infections in Previously Healthy Persons - United States*, 31 MORBIDITY AND MORTALITY WEEKLY REPORT 294 (1982); Centers for Disease Control, *Update on Acquired Immunodeficiency Syndrome (AIDS) - United States*, 31 MORBIDITY AND MORTALITY WEEKLY REPORT 507 (1982); Centers for Disease Control, *Unexplained Immunodeficiency and Opportunistic Infections in Infants - New York, New Jersey and California*, 31 MORBIDITY AND MORTALITY WEEKLY REPORT 665 (1982).
17. Chicago Trib. *supra* note 14, at 12.

Figure 1. AIDS Cases per 100,000 Population by State Reported from January to December 1990

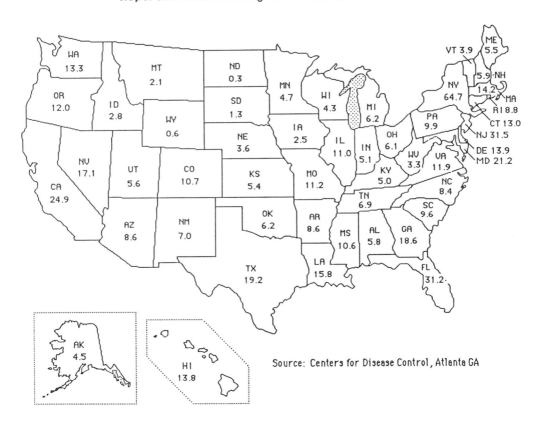

Source: Centers for Disease Control, Atlanta GA

making it difficult to diagnose the disease early in its development. Symptoms may closely resemble other lymphatic diseases, such as mononucleosis, making it difficult to identify the virus without the aid of blood tests. Much of the information regarding the symptoms of HIV infection has originated from case studies involving newly infected individuals. An Australian study reported that victims experienced fever, fatigue, muscle aches, joint pains, head aches, loss of appetite, nausea, sore throat, diarrhea, sweats, swollen glands and a rash within 3 to 14 days after exposure to the AIDS virus through another infected individual.[18] The symptoms quickly disappear, and the disease is dormant within the individual, often for years. When activated, the AIDS virus systematically disables the immune system making the person vulnerable to various diseases and opportunistic infections which ultimately bring about death.

The debate still rages, however, as to the specific causes and transmission of the deadly disease. Despite a three billion dollar a year battle against the AIDS virus, a vaccine or cure is still unknown. "In the absence of any drug that can kill HIV without killing the body that harbors it, scientists leading the fight against AIDS see the result as inevitable: Once you are infected, your body cannot kill the virus. The virus eventually destroys the immune system. You die."[19]

AIDS Within the School Setting

The public has become overtly concerned with the possibility of HIV transmission within the school setting particularly at the elementary and preschool level where children often exchange bodily fluids or bite each other.[20] Although available scientific information suggests that there is a low risk of HIV transmission among children within the educational environment, public health officials admit their experience with AIDS among children is limited. Because the social hysteria associated with the disease is rife, the public is demanding that the scientific community provide absolute evidence regarding HIV transmission potentials. Informational and technological inadequacies within the scientific community, however, make this task impossible. Any information regarding the AIDS virus or its transmission potential must be examined within the full perspective of cur-

---

18. Cooper, Maclean, Finlayson, Michelmore, Gold, Donovan, Barnes, Brooke and Penny, *Acute AIDS Retrovirus Infection: Definition of a Clinical Illness Associated with Seroconversion*, 1 LANCET 537 (1985).
19. Burkett, Miami Herald, Dec. 23, 1990, at 13.
20. Rogers, *AIDS in Children: A Review of the Clinical Epidemiologic and Public Health Aspects*, 4 PED. INF. DIS. 230 (1985).

rent scientific research. To do less would proliferate one of the most devastating societal factors associated with the AIDS epidemic—ignorance.

Public schools are an important environment epidemiologically because of the proximity that inherently exists within their boundaries. The daily interaction of large numbers of individuals within a small environment provides an efficient mechanism for the rapid deployment of disease. Schools have historically been the environmental agents in the transmission of many highly infectious diseases, such as chicken pox, epidemic parotitis (mumps), influenza, rubella (German measles), and rubeola (measles). Although the transmission risks associated with AIDS remain low, the question of whether children with AIDS should be allowed to attend school has generated a great deal of controversy.

The low transmission risk posited by CDC officials for school children is a conclusion not supported by all members of the scientific community. In his position as professor of medicine at the New York State Medical School, Giron argues that the risk associated with HIV transmission may be higher for children in school because they are often the victims of cuts, abrasions, nose bleeds, and human bites. Although there currently has been no documented case of HIV transmission between infected and healthy school children, the possibility cannot be overlooked.[21] Researchers at CDC have stated that the scientific data concerning younger and neurologically handicapped children are very limited. Realizing this limitation, they recommend the following:

> For the infected pre-school aged child and for some neurologically handicapped children who lack control of their bodily secretions or who display behavior such as biting, and those children who have uncoverable, oozing lesions, a more restrictive environment is advisable until more is known about transmission in these settings. Children infected with HTLV-III/LAV (HIV) should be cared for and educated in settings that minimize exposure of other children to blood or body fluids.[22]

Medical experts suggest that in determinations regarding the educational placement of HIV-positive children, decision makers should consider the child's emotional, physical, and neurological conditions and the decision should be made cooperatively by a group consisting of the child's parents

---

21. Giron, *Doctor Wants Teachers Warned of AIDS Pupils*, Los Angeles Times, Sept. 19, 1985, at I18.
22. Centers for Disease Control, *Education and Foster Care of Children Infected with Human T-lymphotropic Virus Type III/Lymphadenopathy Associated Virus*, 34 MORBIDITY AND MORTALITY WEEKLY REPORT 517 (1985).

or guardian, a physician, a public health official, and the school personnel involved.

Knowledge about AIDS and the human immunodeficiency virus continues to expand and improve; thus, decisions about the educational placement and care of HIV-infected students should be based upon the best scientific and medical knowledge available. Considerations include, but are not limited to, the following:

1. the risk to the student including physical condition, immune status, stamina, degree of handicap, and need for any special educational setting or physical care;
2. the possible risk to other children or adults that arises from open lesions, infections, inimical behavior, including biting, spitting, fighting, or mouthing objects, such as toys;
3. the environmental needs of the student in terms of age, maturity level, physical condition, neurological status, including control of body functions, and degree of any handicap;
4. the regular assessment of the need for educational alternatives to mainstreamed placement;
5. the risk of experiencing severe complications from infections such as varicella, tuberculosis, measles, cytomegalovirus and herpes simplex virus;
6. the identification of individuals, including the child's physician, who possesses the qualifications necessary to evaluate whether an infected child poses a risk to others, and also the degree of risk for the child; and
7. the desires of the parent(s) or guardian(s) regarding the proposed educational placement or care of the student.

Once student placement has been determined, common sense health precautions should be taken by all persons who are in charge of the care of the infected child. Centers for Disease Control officials recommend that when possible direct skin contact with body fluids should be avoided. Disposable gloves, aprons, and resuscitation mouthpieces should be strategically located and available for use in areas where need is anticipated or possible, such as the office of the nurse, athletic coach, custodian, or site administrator. Nonsterile disposable gloves should be worn when handling blood, such as providing care for nosebleeds, bleeding gums, cuts or wounds; when handling blood-soiled items, such as menstrual pads, bandages or clothing; or when in contact with bodily secretions, such as from open sores. Gloves should also be worn when changing diapers or when handling vomitus, mucous, urine, or feces. Gloves should be changed after use. Care should be taken not to contaminate the environment with soiled gloves or materials. Persons with chapped or cracked skin, eczema, sores, cuts or wounds should be particularly cautious when handling bodily fluids or materials. If extensive contact with body fluids is made, hands should be washed immediately afterwards.[23]

Centers for Disease Control officials further recommend that a thorough review of current procedures for the removal of blood or other body fluids, such as vomitus and feces, should be conducted by public school officials to determine whether appropriate cleaning and disinfection steps have been included. An intermediate level disinfectant, such as isopropyl alcohol, 3% phenolic germicidal detergent, sodium hypochlorite, quaternary ammonium germicidal detergent, or iodophor germicidal detergent, that destroys vegetative bacteria, fungi, tubercle bacillus, and viruses should be used to clean surfaces and materials contaminated with blood or other body fluids.[24] A hypochlorite solution composed of 10 parts water to 1 part bleach is the preferred disinfectant when laundering contaminated clothing or when cleaning objects that may be placed in the mouth.[25]

The incubation period for the AIDS virus may range as high as 4.5 years.[26] The extended incubation period associated with the AIDS virus undoubtedly complicates the efforts of school officials to minimize the transmission potential and to identify children that are infected with HIV prior to their entry into school. Ostensibly, it is possible for a child to become infected with the AIDS virus and not develop antibodies to the disease. Currently, there is a blood test that detects antibodies to the AIDS virus that causes the disease. Antibodies are produced by the immune system when the body tries to eliminate bacteria, viruses, or anything else that is not supposed to be in the bloodstream. The blood test tells the physician if someone has been infected with the AIDS virus. Most people with AIDS have a positive antibody test and some people with a positive antibody test will develop AIDS. A program of blood screening would be ineffective in recognizing HIV infection in these children because tests, such as the enzyme-linked immunosorbent assay (ELISA) and the Western blot, are only sensitive to the presence of viral antibodies. The test does not indicate who will develop AIDS.

---

23. UNIVERSITY OF MIAMI, JACKSON MEMORIAL HOSPITAL, CHILDREN'S CLINICAL IMMUNOLOGY UNIT, PRECAUTIONS MANUAL (1988).
24. Martin, McDougal and Loskoski, (1985) *Disinfection and Inactivation of the T-lymphotropic Virus Type-III/Lymphadenopathy Associated Virus*, 152 J. INFECT. DIS. 400 (1985) *and see* Spire, Barre-Sinoussi, Montagnieer, and Chermann, *Inactivation of the Lymphadenopathy Associated Virus by Chemical Disinfectants*, 1 LANCET 899 (1984).
25. Centers for Disease Control, *Recommendations for Prevention of HIV Transmission*, 36 MORBIDITY AND MORTALITY WEEKLY REPORTS 1S (1987).
26. Lui, Lawrence, Meade, Morgan, Peterman, Haverkos, and Bregman, *A Model-Based Approach for Estimating Mean Incubation Period of Transfusion-Associated Acquired Immunodeficiency Syndrome*, 83 ANNALS INT. MED. 3051 (1986).

Public health officials note that the immunologic abnormalities associated with symptomatic HIV infection have raised concerns regarding the immunization of children.[27] Immunization of these infected children may produce serious adverse effects. Based on this information, public health officials recommend-

> Live-virus and live-bacterial vaccines (e.g. MMR, OPV) should not be given to children and young adults who are immunosuppressed in association with AIDS or other clinical manifestations of HTLV-III/LAV (HIV) infection. For routine immunizations, these persons should receive inactivated polio vaccine (IPV) and should be excused for medical reasons from regulations requiring measles, rubella, and/or mumps immunization.[28]

Public health officials also recommend that children who are born to women who are at risk of HIV infection or are known to be infected with HIV should undergo serological examination for the AIDS virus. As there is little information currently available on the safety and efficacy of immunizing children who may be infected with HIV, public school officials should apply the CDC vaccination guidelines with students known to be infected with HIV as well as those at high risk of being infected with HIV whose serological status is unknown.

Public awareness of AIDS has been as profound as the anxiety it has created. Public misconception about this disease has kindled a firestorm of fear and controversy that has swept the country over the last few years. The fact that present scientific and medical evidence suggests that HIV cannot be casually transmitted has not ameliorated public fears concerning AIDS. As a result, a sizable portion of the American public still believes that the scientific community has underestimated the transmission potential of this disease, particularly in the case of public schools. Arguably, the fact that HIV has been isolated in a significant number of bodily fluids, many of which could be exchanged through everyday circumstances, lends support for this line of reasoning. Minimally, it suggests that perhaps some possibility of transmission still exists for this infectious agent. Regardless of what is already known about AIDS, prominent members of the scientific community have been reticent to state emphatically that the casual communication risks associated with AIDS or HIV are nonexistent. Perhaps the only litmus test available for these conclusions will be the passage of time.

---

27. Centers for Disease Control, *Immunization of Children Infected with Human T-lymphotropic Virus, Type III/Lymphadenopathy Associated Virus*, 35 MORBIDITY AND MORALITY WEEKLY REPS. 595 (1986).
28. *Id.* at 603.

Based upon what is currently known about AIDS, the greatest potential for acquiring or transmitting the AIDS virus within the school environment seems to exist in those circumstances where a person could be exposed to blood or other bodily fluids. Ostensibly, public health officials believe this is possible in situations involving younger children or neurologically handicapped individuals who lack control over their body secretions, who possess uncoverable sores or lesions, or who are prone to inimical behavior. Because so little information is available on the issue, public health officials have issued specific recommendations concerning the placement of HIV seropositive children within the educational environment. The promulgation of these recommendations has given the public the impression that AIDS can be communicated, if not everywhere, then at least within the public school setting. Given the possibility that between one and two million Americans carry HIV asymptomatically, the threat of AIDS becomes quite real to the public. The realization that some of these infected individuals may reside undetected within schools for years certainly augments the level of fear that already exists concerning AIDS.

Public fear and doubt about AIDS will probably exist until such time that a viable vaccine, treatment or cure is developed. It is important to realize, in the mean time, that the information concerning AIDS and its underlying cause is continually evolving, often amid controversy. Educational policy, therefore, should reflect a keen awareness of any change that would alter present scientific understanding of AIDS or its transmission potential within public schools. Whenever public opinion and emotions are involved, as with AIDS, issues often require legal resolutions. The legal resolutions necessary to answer many of the problems created by the AIDS epidemic will undoubtedly be as novel as the disease itself.

CHAPTER III
LEGAL IMPLICATIONS OF AIDS
FOR PUBLIC SCHOOLS

Under the provisions of the tenth amendment to the Constitution, states are granted the specific authority to prescribe reasonable rules and regulations to promote and protect the general safety, health, and welfare of its citizens. The critical nature of the epidemic disease phenomenon has prompted many states to exercise their police power to assist communities in peril. Historically, the utilization of police power has been an effective means to forestall the spread of infectious diseases. In terms of social impact, it is extremely difficult to estimate the number of human lives that have been spared in utilizing this constitutionally implied power.

The antecedents of modern public health law arose from the fires of controversy that were kindled by the utilization of police power to combat the periodic incidence of epidemic diseases, such as smallpox,[1] leprosy,[2] cholera,[3] bubonic plague,[4] scarlet fever,[5] tuberculosis,[6] and venereal disease[7] that have occurred in this country within the last century. The hallmark of many of these cases is the latitude that was consistently afforded to the state legislatures by the courts. In many instances, state actions were presumed to be valid because of the compelling nature of the public interest involved. In this context, personal rights were often considered subordinate to the interests of the state. Even in those circumstances where personal freedom was severely attenuated by a particular legislative action, courts were averse to making determinations that would substitute their own judgment for that of the legislature. Regardless of this, there are many people who view the utilization of police power as a serious threat

---

1. Harrison v. Mayor and City Council of Baltimore, 1 Gill 264 (Md. 1843); Beckwith v. Sturdevant, 42 Conn. 158 (1875); Spring v. Inhabitants of Hyde Park, 137 Mass. 554, 50 Am. Rep. 334 (1884); City of Richmond v. Henrico County Superv., 83 Va. 204, 2 S.E. 26 (1887); Smith v. Emery, 42 N.Y.S. 258, 11 App. Div. 10 (1896); Henderson County Bd. of Health v. Ward, 107 Ky. 477, 54 S.W. 725 (1900); Hengehold v. City of Covington, 108 Ky. 752, 57 S.W. 495 (1900); Highland v. Schulte, 82 N.W. 62 (Mich. 1900); Allison v. Cash, 137 S.W. 245 (Ky. 1911); Crayton v. Larrabee, 220 N.Y. 493, aff'd 147 N.Y.S. 1105 (N.Y. 1917).
2. Kirk v. Wyman, 83 S.C. 372, 65 S.E. 387 (S.C. 1909).
3. Rudolphe v. City of New Orleans, 11 La. Ann. 242 (1854).
4. Jew Ho v. Williamson, 103 F. Supp. 10 (N.D. Cal. 1900).
5. People v. Tait, 102 N.E. 750 (Ill. 1913); State v. Rackowski, 86 A. 606 (Conn. 1913).
6. White v. Seattle Local Union No. 81, 337 P.2d 289 (Wash. 1959); Jones v. Czapkay, 6 Cal Rptr. 182 (1960); Greene v. Edwards, 265 S.E. 2d 662 (W.Va. 1980).
7. State ex rel. McBride v. Superior Ct., 103 Wash. 409 (1918); City of Little Rock v. Smith, 204 P. 364 (1922); State ex rel. Kennedy v. Head, 185 S.W.2d 530 (Tenn. 1945).

to personal liberty. To these individuals, the image of the state as a warrior wielding a sword of police power engaged in mortal combat with some pathogenic adversary does not conform to their concept of state jurisdiction or protection.

The fourteenth amendment to the Constitution expressly states: "No State shall deprive any person of life, liberty, or property, without due process of law; nor deny to any person within its jurisdiction the equal protection of the laws." Individuals who hold this view believe that the issues associated with the use of police power in controlling disease should be deliberated under the rubric of equal protection.

This premise was tested as early as 1905 in *Jacobson v. Massachusetts*[8] when the Supreme Court reviewed a state compulsory immunization statute enacted to avert a possible smallpox epidemic. In its defense, the state presented evidence that confirmed the efficacy of compulsory immunization programs in foreign countries. The Court upheld the action as a valid exercise of state police power finding that public interest must take precedence over individual liberty in circumstances involving public health, safety, and welfare.[9] In presenting its conclusions, the *Jacobson* Court stated:

> We are not prepared to hold that a minority, residing or remaining in any city or town where smallpox is prevalent and enjoying the general protection afforded by an organized local government, may thus defy the will of its constituted authorities, acting in good faith for all, under the legislative sanction of the State. If such be the privilege of a minority then a like privilege would belong to each individual of the community and the spectacle would be presented of the welfare and safety of an entire population being subordinated to the notions of a single individual who chooses to remain part of that population.[10]

The issues raised in *Jacobson* highlight some of the legal difficulties encountered when analyzing equal protection claims. Throughout its tenure, the Supreme Court has been responsive to the reality that specific groups have been subjected to varying degrees of prejudice and discrimination. The idea that specific groups should be afforded greater legal protection began in 1938 when Justice Stone defined a suspect class as a "discrete and insular minority" that is removed from the political process.[11] Stone further suggested that "prejudice against discrete and insular minorities may

---

8. 197 U.S. 11, 24 S. Ct. 358, 49 L.Ed. 643 (1905).
9. *Id.* at 26 *and see* Rochin v. California, 342 U.S. 165, 72 S. Ct. 205, 96 L.Ed. 183 (1952).
10. *Id.* at 37-38.
11. United States v. Carolene Products Co., 304 U.S. 144 (1938).

be a special condition, which tends to curtail the operation of those political processes ordinarily relied upon to protect minorities, and which may be call for a correspondingly more searching judicial inquiry.''[12]

Historically, a number of criteria have been utilized by the courts in qualifying a group as suspect. To be considered as a suspect class, the group must exhibit a long history of victimization by discrimination. It must have an immutable trait that distinguishes the group from others, and it must exhibit stereotypical characteristics that are unrelated to the abilities of the group.[13] Classifications involving race, alienage, national origin, gender, and age have met the criteria necessary to be considered a suspect class.[14]

The court may choose three levels of scrutiny when reviewing regulations that allegedly violate the equal protection clause of the fourteenth amendment. The court will select a level of scrutiny that is consistent with the "character of the discrimination and its relation to legitimate aims.''[15] State regulations that impinge upon a fundamental constitutional right or discriminate against an individual on the basis of a suspect classification are analyzed by the Supreme Court under strict scrutiny. To defend an action successfully under strict scrutiny, the state must demonstrate the existence of a compelling interest and the fact that no less restrictive alternatives are available to those individuals affected by the action.[16].

In circumstances where a classification does not meet the criteria necessary to trigger strict scrutiny, but still results in recurrent constitutional difficulties, the state's action will be reviewed under an intermediate level of scrutiny as exemplified in *Plyer v. Doe*.[17] Intermediate scrutiny has proven to be an effective analytical tool within the fields of public health and education where it has been used to substantiate the existence of either personal rights or suspect classifications that have yet to become firmly established within the context of constitutional law. Intermediate scrutiny, as an analytical tool, may be regarded as a legal hybrid of the rational basis and strict scrutiny tests. Under intermediate scrutiny, the state must demonstrate that the disputed measure has a "substantial" relationship to

---

12. *Id.* at 152, n. 4.
13. Fronterio v. Richardson, 411 U.S. 677 (1973); Patida, *AIDS: Do Children With AIDS Have a Right to Attend School?* 13 PEPPERDINE L. REV. 1041 (1986).
14. City of Cleburne v. Cleburne Living Center, 105 S. Ct. 3249 (1985); YUDOF, KIRP, VAN GEEL AND LEVIN, EDUCATIONAL POLICY AND THE LAW: CASES AND MATERIALS (1982).
15. Matthews v. Lucas, 427 U.S. 495 (1976) at 504.
16. Korematsu v. United States, 323 U.S. 214 (1944); Sherbert v. Verner, 374 U.S. 398; 83 S. Ct. 1790, 10 L.Ed.2d 965 (1963); Dunn v. Blumstein, 405 U.S. 330 (1972).
17. 457 U.S. 202 (1982).

a legitimate state interest and represents the least restrictive means available to attain that goal.

In instances where neither strict nor intermediate scrutiny is appropriate, the state action is reviewed under minimum scrutiny or what is referred to as the rational basis test. Under minimum scrutiny, the state action is presumed valid unless proven to be arbitrary or capricious or it exhibits no reasonable relationship to a legitimate state interest.[18]

States have successfully defended the utilization of police power in circumstances involving communicable disease on the basis of several criteria: the number of people actually or potentially affected, the severity of the disease, or the possible economic consequences to society. Regardless of the criteria the state uses to support its position, the mortality often associated with contagious diseases remains the most compelling of state interests.

Jacobson provided an important vehicle for states to exercise their police power in matters pertaining to the health of public school children. In *Hartman v. May*[19] the court upheld a Mississippi ordinance that required children to be vaccinated against smallpox prior to school admission. Unlike many other cases that dealt with compulsory immunization programs for children, this case is notable because of the timing of the ordinance.[20] At the time the ordinance was promulgated, there was no reported outbreak of smallpox. The court considered, however, the epidemic potential of the disease to be ample justification for the state's action. Additional support for state required vaccinations is found in *Pierce v. Board of Education*[21] where a New York court reasoned:

> The experience of the race has taught, to protect the health of the community, to protect the health of man, precautions must be taken against the spread of disease, and vaccination is to prevent not only sickness of the person not vaccinated, but consequences to those with whom such a person might come into contact.[22]

The importance of disease prevention through vaccination has prompted all states to require that children be immunized for diphtheria, measles, rubella, and polio prior to public school entry.[23] Immunization programs

---

18. L. Tribe, American Constitutional Law (1978). *See also* Yudof, Kirp, Van Geel and Levin, Educational Policy and the Law: Cases and Materials (1982).

19. 168 Miss. 477, 151 So. 737 (Miss. 1934).

20. *See also* Allen v. Ingalls, 182 Ark. 991, 33 S.W.2d 1099 (Ark. 1930).

21. Pierce v. Board of Educ., 30 Misc. 2d 1039, 219 N.Y.S.2d 519 (App. Div. 1961).

22. *Id.* at 1040.

23. Department Of Health, Education, and Welfare, Food Service Sanitation Manual, (DHEW Publication No. FDA 78-2081, 1978) at 1.

for children, nevertheless, have been continually attacked under an equal protection analysis arguing that the compulsory nature of such programs affects only those children eligible to attend school. Adults and younger children do not fall under the program's control. Regardless, state courts have consistently rejected this argument under provisions of police power. As a result, state mandated health programs for public schools have historically been viewed with minimum scrutiny by the courts. The apparent success of many public school health regulations may be attributed to the unique circumstances that exist in the educational environment that make them highly efficient mechanisms for the communication of disease. This observation has provided a rational basis for a number of state actions involving children.[24]

It has been argued that state prescribed immunization programs for school children are inconsistent with state compulsory education laws and that the imposition of health-related admission requirements deprive children of their property rights to obtain a public education. The courts have rejected both of these arguments under the penumbra of state police power and the necessity for promoting public safety.[25] The importance of public health was clarified in an early case when the court reasoned:

> The welfare of the many is superior to that of the few, and, as the regulations compelling vaccinations are intended to and enforced solely for the public good, the rights conferred thereby are primary and superior to the rights of any pupil to attend public schools.[26]

Although it may appear that the exercise of police power in circumstances pertaining to public health is settled, there remains some rather persuasive legal arguments against state public health intervention. This legal reasoning may have bearing upon the control of AIDS.

Some of the most critical attacks against state imposed health regulations have centered upon the infringement on religious expression.[27] The individual's right to a free exercise of religion is preferentially protected under the provisions of the first amendment to the United States Constitution. The legal dimensions of this constitutional freedom were originally

---

24. Herbert v. Board of Educ., 197 Ala. 617, 73 So. 321 (1916); Zucht v. King, 225 S.W. 267 (Tex. Ct. Civ. App. 1920); Nebbia v. New York, 291 U.S. 502, 54 S. Ct. 505, 78 L.Ed. 940 (1934).
25. Hartman v. May, 168 Miss. 477, 151 So. 737 (1934); Booth v. Board of Educ., 70 S.W.2d 350 (Tex. Civ. App. 1934).
26. Freeman v. Zimmerman, 86 Minn. 353, 90 N.W. 783 (1902) at 361.
27. New Braunsfels v. Waldschmidt, 109 Tex. 302, 207 S.W. 303 (1918); Vonnegut v. Baun, 206 Ind. 172, 188 N.E. 677 (1934); Dunham v. Board of Educ., 154 Ohio 469, 96 N.E.2d 413 (1951); Wright v. DeWitt School Dist., 238 Ark. 906, 385 S.W.2d 644 (1965).

considered to extend only to religious belief.[28]   In an attempt to protect individuals from state interference, a distinction between "religious beliefs" and "actions based on religious beliefs" was made in 1940 when the court in *Cantwell v. Connecticut* concluded that the first amendment protects not only the freedom to believe, but in some circumstances, the freedom to act as well.[29]   The importance of this distinction was tested again in *Wisconsin v. Yoder* when the Court considered the constitutionality of a compulsory attendance law involving a group of Amish children.[30]   The Amish challenge of religious infringement was upheld by the Court in its finding that the state did not demonstrate a compelling interest in requiring the Amish children to stay in school beyond the eighth grade.[31]

The contentions raised by the Amish against compulsory education statutes could be utilized by individuals objecting to state prescribed AIDS regulations.   Religious groups, such as Christian Scientists or Jehovah's Witnesses, could raise deeply-held religious objections to any prescriptive state action requiring either medical screening or treatment for AIDS.   In light of *Yoder*, state legislators have shifted slightly away from the rigid precedent established in *Jacobson* to provide religious exemptions to individuals in circumstances involving minor social hazards.[32]   By applying the strict scrutiny standard to these cases, courts have expanded their analyses to include more of the circumstances associated with state public health regulation while looking for the least restrictive alternative.   In cases involving children where religious objections are presented by the parents, courts have been reluctant to grant exemptions because of the state's overriding interest in preventing the spread of disease and protecting the health of the child.[33]   Although the granting of exemptions for religious objectors appears to be gratuitous in nature, these exemptions suggest that a subtle change has occurred in legal and legislative thinking which may indicate a less compelling interest on the part of the state.   This change may become more pronounced in the future, thereby complicating state efforts to regulate public health in response to the AIDS dilemma.   Persons who oppose state required medical practices and cannot base their objections on religious principles may see remedy through the constitutional right of privacy.[34]   Although not specifically enumerated in the Constitution, the Supreme Court does recognize its importance.   In 1981, the

---

28. United States v. Reynolds, 98 U.S 145, 25 L.Ed. 244 (1878).
29. 310 U.S. 296, 60 S. Ct. 900, 84 L.Ed. 1213 (1040).
30. 406 U.S. 205, 92 S. Ct. 1526, 32 L.Ed.2d 15 (1972).
31. *Id.* at 224.
32. Dalli v. Board of Educ., 358 Mass. 753, 267 N.E.2d 219 (1971).
33. Jehovah's Witnesses v. King County Hosp., 278 F. Supp. 183 (S.D.N.Y. 1968).
34. Dover, *An Evaluation of Immunization Regulation in Light of Religious Objections and the Developing Right of Privacy*, 4 UNIV. DAYTON L. REV. 401 (1979).

Court stated in *Union Pacific Railway v. Botsford*:

> No right is held more sacred, or is more carefully guarded by the common law, than the right of every individual to the possession and control of his own person, free from restraint or interference of others unless by clear and unquestionable authority of law.[35]

The emergence of the right of privacy continued in *Meyer v. Nebraska* where the concept was broadened somewhat under the fourteenth amendment.[36] It was not until 1965, however, when the Supreme Court decided *Griswold v. Connecticut* that the right to privacy garnered substantial support for consideration as a constitutional liberty emanating from the Bill of Rights.[37] In this case, the Court found the state's action unconstitutional under the strict scrutiny standard. Despite this fact, case law in other constitutional areas reveals that the liberty rights enjoyed by persons in this country are not absolute. In *Roe v. Wade*, the Supreme Court indicated that the right to personal privacy was an inherently fundamental constitutional liberty, but may be limited by the compelling state interest in protecting the public from the spread of communicable diseases.[38] The legal issues concerning personal privacy have been a recurring theme throughout judicial history demonstrating the importance of this fundamental personal liberty.

Decisions associated with the personal right to privacy could have a significant impact upon future legislation where state police power is utilized to require involuntary physical examinations and treatment for victims of contagious diseases.[39] In the past, states have attempted to employ this method of disease control in cases involving prostitution and sexually transmitted diseases.[40] When subjected to the rational basis test, a state could argue that specific modes of personal conduct, such as prostitution or homosexuality, are subject to greater control because they can be linked directly to the transmission of venereal diseases.[41] This line of reasoning was tested in *Wragg v. Griffin* involving the forced examination of prostitutes under the suspicion that they were carriers of venereal

---

35. 141 U.S. 250, 11 S. Ct. 1000, 35 L.Ed. 734 (1981) at 253.
36. 262 U.S. 390, 43 S. Ct. 625, 67 L.Ed. 1042 (1923).
37. 381 U.S. 479, 85 S. Ct. 1678, 13 L.Ed.2d 510 (1965).
38. 410 U.S. 113, 93 S. Ct. 705, 35 L.Ed.2d 147 (1973).
39. Speigel, *Privacy, Sodomy, AIDS and the Schools: Case Studies in Equal Protection*. AN-NUAL SURV. AM. L. 221 (1986).
40. Prentice and Murray, *Liability for Transmissions of Herpes: Using Traditional Tort Principles to Encourage Honesty in Sexual Relationships*, 11 J. CONTEMP. L. 67 (1984).
41. Parmet, *AIDS and Quarantine; The Revival of an Archaic Doctrine*, 14 HOFSTRA L. REV. 76 (1985); Petteway, *Compulsory Quarantine and Treatment of Persons With Venereal Disease*, 18 FLA. L. J. 13 (1944).

diseases.[42] The court decided in favor of plaintiff prostitutes by stating: "Nowhere does the law provide for the deprivation of liberty of a person without due process of law by forcing an examination on mere suspicion."[43] This line of reasoning will undoubtedly impact any similar legislative action promulgated in response to the AIDS crisis. Ostensibly, the concept of personal freedom is so woven into the constitutional fabric of this nation that to abridge that freedom necessitates more than "mere suspicion" that a danger to society exists.

In those circumstances where suspicion escalated into eminent danger, states often exerted their police authority to institute measures that would quickly isolate disease carriers from the remainder of the general population.[44] In terms of efficacy, quarantines represent an effective weapon in the arsenal of public health regulations utilized by state health officials to combat the spread of infectious diseases. The obvious purpose behind the use of a quarantine is to minimize the further transmission of a potentially epidemic contagion by restricting one or more individuals to a specific building or area. In considering quarantines as a method of disease control, many legal observers believe that quarantines are unconstitutional because they deprive individuals of their freedom without due process of law. This position was substantiated in *Jew Ho v. Williamson* when the Ninth Circuit Court of Appeals stepped in to invalidate a quarantine action by San Francisco public health officials involving 15,000 people.[45]. The court held that the quarantine was "discriminating in its character, and...contrary to the provisions of the 14th Amendment of the Constitution of the United States."[46]

Although the constitutionality of quarantines suffered an early defeat, some states were unwilling to relinquish what they perceived to be an effective weapon in the war against infectious diseases. In *People ex rel. Barmore v. Robertson*, the use of a quarantine to control the spread of typhoid fever was held by the court to be reasonable in light of the epidemic nature of the typhoid virus.[47] In its conclusion, the court stated:

> One of the important elements in the administration of health
> and quarantine regulation is a full measure of common sense. It
> is not necessary for health authorities to wait until the person
> affected with a contagious disease has actually caused others

---

42 184 Iowa 243, 170 N.W. 400 (1919).
43. *Id.* at 247.
44. Gleason, *Quarantine: An Unreasonable Solution to the AIDS Dilemma*, 55 CIN. L. REV. 217 (1986).
45. 103 F. Supp. 10 (N.D. Cal. 1900).
46. *Id.* at 26.
47. 302 Ill. 422, 134 N.E. 815 (1922).

to become sick by contact with him before he is placed under quarantine.[48]

The judgment in this case generated considerable debate within the legal community because many individuals found the court's decision to incarcerate individuals without knowledge of their health status to be incongruous with what should represent a "full measure of common sense." In subsequent cases, the apparent reasonableness of the state's position regarding quarantines quickly waned in light of *Wragg* which prohibited public health regulation on the basis of suspicion.

The issues associated with quarantines have surfaced again in response to the AIDS epidemic. Public health and law enforcement officials alike have been frustrated by their inability to control the actions of people infected with the AIDS virus who continue to be involved in prostitution. Although people may have some legal recourse after becoming infected with a contagious disease through sexual contact with a prostitute or known disease carrier, there is as yet no legal precedent that would prevent this type of personal assault. The fact that AIDS is a fatal disease has prompted some persons to seek the charge of involuntary manslaughter in response to the magnitude of the attack. It would seem impractical, however, to apply civil and criminal statutes to these circumstances because of the variability observed in the dormancy of the AIDS virus and the difficulty of confirming the exclusivity of the sexual relationship between the victim and the infected partner.

The importance of obtaining accurate information about the transmission potential of the AIDS virus and its relative danger to the general public before attempting to legislate health regulations has been adequately demonstrated in the case of antifornication laws promulgated to control the spread of herpes and other contagious venereal diseases. The fact that AIDS is somewhat analogous to genital herpes, even though herpes is not fatal, has prompted many state legislatures in need of an AIDS policy to draw parallels between the two. Attempts have been made to control the spread of communicable diseases through the enactment of antifornication statutes which carry criminal penalties.[49] Even though antifornication statutes have been justified under the provisions of police power, they have been attacked continuously in the courts, as are sodomy statutes. The impact of these statutes have done little to prevent the spread of contagious diseases and may actually frustrate state efforts to control them. This belief was expressed in *State v. Saunders*.[50], when the court stated:

---

48. *Id.* at 434.
49. Nicols, *AIDS — A New Reason to Regulate Homosexuality?* 11 J. CONTEMP. L. 315 (1984).
50. 74 N.J. 200, 381 A.2d 333 (1977).

If the State's interest in the instant statute is that it is helpful in preventing venereal disease, we conclude that it is counter productive. To the extent that any successful program to combat venereal disease must depend upon affected persons coming forward for treatment, the present statute operates as a deterrent to such voluntary participation. The fear of being prosecuted for the 'crime' of fornication can only deter people from seeking such necessary treatment.[51]

The issue of reporting is particularly important in the fight against AIDS. As part of a national effort to curtail the spread of epidemic disease, every state has enacted legislation that requires the reporting of specific diseases, such as AIDS, to public health officials.[52] The reporting and analysis of scientific data pertaining to the epidemiological distribution of disease are recognized as necessary components of the disease control process. Nonetheless, the collection of epidemiological information has been challenged on constitutional grounds as an invasion of personal privacy.[53] An examination of case law on this point reveals that mandatory disease reporting has generally been upheld by the judiciary as a legal exercise of state police power "so long as the information sought is reasonably related to a legitimate health purpose and is limited to public health departments, and so long as statutory confidentiality protections are in place."[54] The constitutional controversy associated with the collection of scientific research information came to a focus in *Whalen v. Roe* where the Supreme Court concluded that "limited reporting requirements in the medical field are familiar, and are not generally regarded as an invasion of privacy."[55]

Currently, most states have included an infectious disease reporting provision within their legislative public health packages that focuses specifically upon AIDS. Unfortunately, the medical condition referred to as AIDS does not represent a single clinical illness, rather it encompasses an entire spectrum of clinical manifestations that range from HIV seropositivity to frank clinical AIDS. To avoid confusion and to enhance validity, most states have constructed their AIDS reporting legislation around the surveillance and reporting guidelines that have been issued by the Centers for Disease Control in Atlanta.

---

51. *Id.* at 342.
52. Curran, Gostin, and Clarke, *Acquired Immunodeficiency Syndrome: Legal, Regulatory, and Policy Analysis* (U.S. Dep't of Health and Human Services, No. 282-86-0032, 1986).
53. Heaney, *The Constitutional Rights of Informational Privacy: Does It Protect Children Suffering From AIDS?* 14 FORDHAM URBAN L. J. 927 (1986).
54. Gostin, *Traditional Public Health Strategies* 48 in AIDS AND THE LAW, A GUIDE FOR THE PUBLIC (H. L. Dalton and S. Burris eds. 1987) at 58.
55. 429 U.S. 606 (1977).

In a 1987 investigation of public health strategies, Gostin concluded that a majority of the state legislatures in this country have experienced considerable success in obtaining necessary epidemiological information on AIDS because they have taken steps to narrowly tailor and properly regulate their statutory requirements for infectious disease reporting. By adopting a narrow legal approach, state legislatures have been able to preserve the constitutional validity of the measure by minimizing the privacy problems that have often been associated with other case identification measures, such as mass screening. Proper regulation of a health measure once it has been promulgated protects the confidentiality of personal information and does not deter people with AIDS from seeking competent medical assistance.

Case identification measure that utilize HIV status are more problematic because the collection of such information "could create a skewed epidemiological impression of the total infected population.[56] For the most part, HIV antibody testing in the United States is voluntary and involves rather limited population groups. Conclusions that could be drawn from a statistical analysis of HIV status among these groups would be inaccurate because of inadequate sample size and self-selection. Attempts to improve the validity of the analysis by increasing the sample size through mandatory HIV reporting would not improve the results and could prove to be counterproductive because it would create an environment that would deter health people from investigating their own HIV status. This result would frustrate efforts to control the disease by creating a barrier to AIDS education and counseling.

The fear and hysteria concerning AIDS have made compulsory disease control measures politically and culturally appealing to many individuals within this country. Despite their appeal, Brandt contends that any attempt to control AIDS through compulsory legislative measure will undoubtedly prove to be expensive and may actually serve to augment the AIDS crisis.[57]

Many observers suggest that the problems that are associated with AIDS run much deeper and are far more damaging than originally recognized. The AIDS crisis has been like a small "puncture wound" in the "body" of society. The superficial nature of the wound belies the real damage that exists beneath the skin where organ damage and hemorrhaging threaten the entire body. Charges that the federal government has failed to understand the critical nature of the AIDS crisis and has attempted to ameliorate

---

56. Gostin, *supra* note 54, at 58.
57. Brandt, *AIDS in Historical Perspective: Four Lessons From the History of Sexually Transmitted Diseases*, 78 AM. J. PUB. HEALTH 367 (1988).

the situation by applying a band-aid rather than treating the entire condition have been leveled.[58]

Children with AIDS: An Equal Protection Analysis

The issues associated with AIDS and public schools exist primarily with students rather than adults. Public health officials have indicated that specific informational inadequacies concerning younger children have hampered their ability to evaluate the transmission risks associated with the AIDS virus among children. Their cautionary statements concerning the educational placement of sero-positive children assumes that children are at a greater risk within the educational setting than are adults. Although this distinction between children and adults exists scientifically, the legal precedents that emerge apply to both children and adults equally.

The decade encompassing the 1930's was an important period for communicable disease legislation and litigation. During that period of history, the Supreme Court handed down several important decisions confirming the existence and exercise of state police power in protecting the citizens of this country from communicable diseases. Some observers viewed state activity in public health as an unconstitutional intrusion upon their rights and sought legal remedy within the judicial system under the equal protection clause of the fourteenth amendment. In his analysis of case law in this area, Morgenstern observes that legal deference is usually afforded to legislative judgment in circumstances involving communicable diseases when the state can demonstrate that its actions are rationally related to the achievement of a legitimate state end.[59] Although police power has been used effectively in the control and prevention of smallpox, yellow fever, and tuberculosis through mandatory vaccination programs and in the implementation of quarantines, efforts to control the spread of AIDS have proved to be considerably more difficult than efforts observed in previous epidemic diseases. Many of the facts about the disease still remain a mystery to scientists. This fact, along with society's right to be free from communicable disease, must be considered in the balancing analysis between governmental objectives and the rights of those individuals affected by AIDS.

Balancing these factors under the minimum scrutiny of a rationality test would possibly result in the exclusion of children with AIDS from

---

58. Welker, *Acquired Immunodeficiency Syndrome and Public Schools: Scientific, Legal, and Policy Considerations*, UNIVERSITY MICROFILMS, INC. (1989).

59. Morgenstern, *The Role of the Federal Government in Protecting Citizens From Communicable Diseases*, 47 CINCINNATI L. REV. 537 (1978).

school. To the casual observer, a policy excluding AIDS victims from the educational environment would appear to be the most reasonable and expeditious way to protect healthy school children. The freedom enjoyed by victims of AIDS, however, has been seriously jeopardized by the social hysteria that now exists, suggesting that a higher standard of judicial review may be necessary to preserve constitutional liberties.

The ability to protect children with AIDS from state actions that would limit their constitutional rights hinges upon the level of scrutiny applied by the court. As discussed previously, a court may choose from three levels of scrutiny in reviewing regulations that allegedly violate the equal protection clause of the fourteenth amendment. The choice depends upon the nature of the challenged action. State health regulations that exclude children with AIDS from attending school with their peers may qualify for judicial review under strict scrutiny if it can be shown that the regulation limits a fundamental constitutional right or negatively impacts a suspect class of people. Once strict scrutiny has been initiated, the state will carry the burden of proving that its classification is necessary to promote a compelling governmental interest, and that it is precisely and narrowly tailored to serve a legitimate state objective.[60]

The concept of personal liberty emanates both explicitly and implicitly from the Constitution. This belief was reiterated in 1982 when the Supreme court stated that a "fundamental right" is a right that is founded upon the express terms of the Constitution or which may necessarily be implied from those terms.[61] In addressing the legal dilemma faced by children with AIDS, it becomes necessary to determine whether education rises to the level of a fundamental right. In *Brown* the Court stated:

> Education is perhaps the most important function of state and local governments. Compulsory school attendance laws and the great expenditures for education both demonstrate our recognition of the importance of education to our democratic society....It is the very foundation of good citizenship....In these days, it is doubtful that any child may reasonably be expected to succeed in life if he is denied the opportunity of an education.[62]

Despite its sociological importance, the Supreme Court in *San Antonio Independent School District v. Rodriquez* ruled that education is not a fundamental right.[63] It is, therefore, "not among the rights afforded

---

60. Plyer v. Doe, 457 U.S. 202 (1971) at 217.
61. *Id.* at 217, n. 15.
62. Brown v. Board of Educ., 347 U.S. 483 at 493.
63. 411 U.S. 1 (1973).

explicit protection under our Federal Constitution.[64] The legal impact of this decision effectively removes one basis for applying the strict scrutiny standard to state regulations that allegedly discriminate against children with AIDS. Governmental regulations that operate to exclude automatically children with AIDS from school would appear, however, to fit the definition of what constitutes a suspect classification.

On the surface, it would appear that government regulations that classify all children with AIDS or HIV infection similarly by barring them from school would qualify this group as a suspect class. In the short time that society has been confronted with this disease, it is obvious that children with AIDS represent a clearly defined group possessing the immutable characteristic of being infected with a deadly epidemic disease. As a result of their condition, children with AIDS have been subjected to varying degrees of prejudice and discrimination which have isolated them from the general population. From a political perspective, Sotto contends that children with AIDS are particularly vulnerable as a group because they possess no voting power, the majority are members of a racial or ethnic minority, and most have at least one parent that is infected with AIDS.[65] Given these characteristics, it would certainly appear that children with AIDS do fit the image of a suspect class. Upon closer inspection, however, one observes that these children are not without political representation. As AIDS began to expand into the general population, various individuals and organizations surfaced to champion the rights of children afflicted with AIDS. Perhaps their greatest support comes from the opinions expressed by government public health officials who believe that children with AIDS should be allowed to attend public school with their peers.

The existence of political support has proven to be a fatal characteristic for a group to possess when seeking judicial consideration as a suspect class. This line of reasoning was demonstrated in *City of Cleburne v. Cleburne Living Center*[66] where the Supreme Court ruled that individuals diagnosed as mentally retarded do not constitute a suspect class because they are sufficiently represented within the political community. Presumably under a similar analysis, children with AIDS could also be excluded from strict scrutiny because they no longer represent a discrete and insular minority.

The reluctance of the Supreme Court to identify any new group as suspect will undoubtedly continue for some time to come, thereby com-

---

64. *Id.* at 35.
65. Sotto, *Undoing a Lesson of Fear in the Classroom: The Legal Recourse of AIDS-Linked Children*, 135 PA. L. REV. 193 (1986).
66. 105 S. Ct. 3249 (1985).

plicating efforts to protect the rights of children with AIDS. In those instances where neither the rational basis test nor strict scrutiny is appropriate, the Court may utilize an intermediate level of scrutiny to assess the constitutionality of governmental actions. In the past, intermediate scrutiny has been an important legal device for examining equal protection claims involving governmental interference in child rearing[67] and in restricted access to education.[68]

The cases involving educational access are particularly germane to the dilemma faced by children with AIDS. Because education is not considered a fundamental right protected under the fourteenth amendment, children with AIDS could be excluded from public school by regulations that could be upheld under a rational basis test. However, there is legal evidence to indicate that an intermediate level of deference has been applied to educational cases involving restricted access. Most of the evidence for intermediate scrutiny can be observed in *Plyer*, which focused upon a Texas statute prohibiting the children of illegal aliens from attending public school. Although these children were not considered a suspect class nor was education considered to be a fundamental right, the Supreme Court did assert that education was more than just a "benefit indistinguishable from other forms of social legislation."[69] On this basis, the Court ruled that the statutory denial of an education to a "discrete class of children not accountable for their disabling status" was unconstitutional. The state could not prove that its interests were substantially related to the achievement of an important governmental objective.[70]

The Court's analysis in *Plyer* demonstrates a heightened judicial awareness on the part of the Court as to the fundamental importance of education and the plight of children excluded through no fault of their own. In writing for the majority, Justice Brennan makes the following comment:

> Public education is not a 'right' granted to individuals by the Constitution. But neither is it merely some governmental 'benefit'. . . Education has a fundamental role in maintaining the fabric of society. We cannot ignore the significant costs borne by our Nation when selected groups are denied the means to absorb the values and skills upon which our social order

---

67. Halderman v. Pennhurst State School and Hosp., 707 F.2d 702 (3d Cir. 1983) (gender and age discrimination); Craig v. Boren, 429 U.S. 190, 197 (1976); Mississippi University for Women v. Hogan, 458 U.S. 718 (1982).
68. *See* Plyer v. Doe, 457 U.S. 202 (1971); Skyler v. Byrne, 727 F.2d 633 (1984).
69. Plyer v. Doe, 457 U.S. 202 (1971) at 221.
70. *Id.* at 223; *see also*, Reed v. Reed, 404 U.S. 71 (1971) *and* Craig v. Boren, 429 U.S. 190 (1976).

rests...(The) denial of education to some isolated group of
children poses an affront to one of the goals of the Equal Protection Clause; the abolition of governmental barriers presenting unreasonable obstacles to advancement on the basis of individual merit.[71]

The opinions presented in *Plyer* become extremely important in the
legal analysis of health regulations aimed at children with AIDS. Like
the children of undocumented aliens in *Plyer*, children with AIDS may
be considered a "quasi-suspect-class" because of their affliction and because
they have been subjected to varying degrees of prejudice. Moreover, education is a right that, if not considered fundamental, at least rises to the level
of a "quasi-fundamental-right" because of its importance to society.
Governmental regulations that are aimed at protecting society from children
with AIDS by excluding them from public school will undoubtedly devastate
the emotional and psychological development of these children unless special
accommodations are granted to them.

State legislatures have occasionally addressed this problem through
the development of home schooling programs. In *Brown* the Supreme Court
concluded "that in the field of public education the doctrine of 'separate
but equal' has no place." Separate educational facilities are inherently
unequal.[72] Although the *Brown* decision focused on racial segregation,
courts since that time have been extremely sensitive to the issue of equal
educational opportunity and most are reticent to accept the premise that
separate education equates with equal education.

In *Plyer* the majority ruled in favor of the children "by patching together bits and pieces of what might be termed as a quasi-suspect-class
and a quasi-fundamental rights analysis."[73] The legality of health regulations that automatically exclude children with AIDS from school will depend substantially upon the communicability of the AIDS virus. In *New
York State Association for Retarded Children, Inc. v. Carey* the court overturned a New York City Board of Education decision to exclude certain
mentally retarded children from school because they were carriers of
hepatitis.[74] The position of the board in this case was seriously eroded
by the fact that the health hazard posed by these children was nothing more
than a remote possibility. In addition, the classification used to exclude
them was under-inclusive in that it failed to consider normal children that
were carriers of hepatitis B as well.[75] In *LaRocca v. Dalsheim*, prison

71. *Id.* at 221.
72. Brown v. Board of Educ., 347 U.S. 483 (1954) at 495.
73. Plyer v. Doe, 457 U.S. 202 (1971) at 244.
74. 612 F.2d 664 (2d Cir. 1979).
75. *Id.* at 649.

inmates sought an injunction against the correctional facility to prevent sero-positive prisoners from being housed or treated at the same prison.[76] The court denied the injunction request on the ground that "as long as the precautions for hepatitis B are followed in the prison," there is no need to remove the prisoners with AIDS from the facility.

Although these two cases represent situations very similar to those facing children with AIDS, the finding in both courts is limited in scope. Even though the risk of acquiring the AIDS virus through casual contact remains low, researchers have detected the presence of the virus in a significant number of body fluids suggesting the possibility that the AIDS virus could be transmitted in ways yet unknown to science. It should be remembered that the virus responsible for AIDS can remain latent, sometimes undetected, within the human body for years. This viral characteristic makes it difficult to test for the presence of the AIDS virus within any one person or population. Furthermore, the analysis in *Carey* focused on hepatitis B, and although it is considered to be a serious disease, it does not possess the fatal characteristics of AIDS. The existence of these differences will enable subsequent courts to reevaluate the circumstances presented in each of the two previous cases using the most reliable scientific data available.

With this caveat aside, based on the prevailing scientific assertion that AIDS is not a casually transmitted disease, an application of the *Plyer* intermediate scrutiny standard would deny the constitutionality of any health regulation that would seek to exclude children with AIDS from school or isolate them from their classmates. Nevertheless, numerous attempts have been made by school officials in New York, New Jersey, Florida, and Indiana to exclude children with AIDS from the educational environment.[77] In one particular instance, the New York Court in *District 27 Community School Board v. Board of Education* found a local school board proposal to exclude children with AIDS in violation of the equal protection clause stating:

> The 'apparent nonexistent risk of transmission of HTLV-III/LAV (HIV)' in the school setting finds strong support in the epidemiological data...and because the automatic exclusion of children with AIDS...would effect a purpose having no adequate connection with public health, it would usurp the function of the Commissioner of Health if this court adjudged...that the non-exclusion policy was arbitrary and

---

76. 120 Misc. 2d 697, 467 N.Y.S.2d 302 (Sup. Ct. 1983).
77. Sotto, *supra* note 64 at 194, n. 8.

capricious simply because in the court of public opinion, that particular policy was . . . not the best choice.[78]

If a court under an equal protection analysis reviews a regulation and observes that neither strict scrutiny nor intermediate scrutiny is applicable, the court will utilize the minimum scrutiny of a rational basis test to determine legality of the regulation in question. Historically, the Supreme Court has granted considerable legislative deference to governmental regulations analyzed under this standard. Recently, the Court has become less tolerant of classification schemes that were not rationally related to a legitimate state purpose.[79] This shift in judicial thinking could prove to be beneficial for the thousands of individuals afflicted with AIDS.

The question remains as to whether it is rational to treat children with AIDS differently than their classmates. Although it is true that children with AIDS suffer from a disability not shared by their peers, does their disability warrant the distinction forced upon them by government regulation, especially in light of the current scientific information available? In *City of Cleburne*, the Supreme Court stated that "the state may not rely on a classification whose relationship to an asserted goal is so attenuated as to render the distinction arbitrary or irrational.[80] In considering the rights of children with AIDS, the prevailing medical and scientific evidence demonstrates that by allowing these children to remain with their schoolmates, their presence within the public school setting would not jeopardize any public interest in preventing the spread of AIDS. In view of this analysis, it then becomes clear that any governmental regulation that automatically attempts to bar children with AIDS from attending public school would fail to meet the requirements of a rational basis test and would subsequently be found unlawful by the courts.

Federal Protection For Individuals with AIDS

For some time, Congress has recognized the special needs of handicapped Americans. Prior to 1973, handicapped members of our society suffered under extreme prejudicial and discriminatory treatment which prevented many of them from enjoying the fullness of life. In speaking to the problems faced by the handicapped in 1973, Senator Dole asserted:

---

78. 130 Misc. 2d 398, 502 N.Y.S.2d (Sup. Ct. 1986) at 435.
79. *See* Hooper v. Bernalillo County Assessor, 105 S. Ct. 2862 (1985) *and* Metropolitan Life Ins. Co. v. Ward, 105 S. Ct. 1676 (1985).
80. City of Cleburne v. Cleburne Living Center, 105 Sup. Ct. 3249 (1985) at 3258.

Along with (the) great potential there is a great need for understanding - of the problems the handicapped face - of the assistance they require to fulfill their potential - and of priorities for the limited resources available to attain this goal. Each person has the common needs of all people. . . . But beyond these basic needs, handicapped people have special requirements to enable them to maximize their potentials for individual, social, and professional development.[81]

To meet the extraordinary needs of the handicapped, Congress enacted the Rehabilitation Act of 1973. Along with the establishment of the Rehabilitation Services Administration, this congressional enactment established specific employment rights for handicapped individuals.[82] One of the major objectives of the Rehabilitation Act, is stated thus:

No otherwise qualified handicapped individual. . .shall, solely by reason of his handicap, be excluded from the participation in, be denied benefits of, or be subject to discrimination under any program or activity receiving federal financial assistance.[83]

Most school systems throughout the United States utilize federal funds to meet the educational and developmental needs of the students they serve. By accepting these funds, public schools become legally bound by proscriptions of the Rehabilitation Act. Although the Rehabilitation Act focuses primarily upon employment discrimination, section 504 is particularly important to children with AIDS because it may provide a legal mechanism for them to assert a right to a regular, nonsegregated education.

The applicability of the Rehabilitation Act to persons with AIDS is dependent upon the meaning that is attached to the term "handicapped individual" using its legal infancy, the Rehabilitation Act focused primarily on employment and vocational rehabilitation services. In 1982, Congress determined that the original focus of the Act was inconsistent with its objective of preventing discrimination. As a result, Congress revised the language of the Act to give it a wider scope of applicability. Under the present definition, a handicapped individual is defined as "any person who (i) has a physical or mental impairment, which substantially limits one or

---

81. 119 CONGR. REC. 24589 (1973) (statement of R. Dole).
82. Dlutowski, *Employment Discrimination: AIDS Victims*, 9 HARV. J.L. & PUB. POL'Y. 739 (1986); Silverstein, *AIDS and Employment: An Epidemic Strikes the Workplace and the Law*, 8 WHITTIER L. REV. 651 (1986).
83. 29 U.S.C. § 706 (1982).

more of such person's major life activities, (ii) has a record of such impairment, or (iii) is regarded as having such an impairment."[84]

The Department of Health and Human Services (HHS) is the government agency responsible for implementing section 504 of the Rehabilitation Act. According to HHS regulations, a physical impairment is broadly defined as a "physiological disorder or condition, cosmetic disfigurement, or anatomical loss affecting one or more of the following body systems: neurological; musculoskeletal; special sense organs; respiratory, including speech organs; cardiovascular; reproductive, digestive, genitourinary; hemic and lymphatic; skin and endocrine."[85] Although the immune system is not explicitly mentioned in the HHS definition, AIDS qualifies as a physical impairment because it is medically recognized as a physiological disorder which affects the hemic and lymphatic systems. It is clear that as the disease progresses the degree to which the individual is handicapped also increases. Eventually, the victim loses the ability to function both physically and psychologically within society.

The Rehabilitation Act also protects the rights of persons who are handicapped by the perceptions of others because they are "regarded as having. . .an impairment."[86] Under this line of reasoning, individuals who are perceived by others as having AIDS are afforded the same protection as those who actually have the disease. Presumably this could include (a) persons having an AIDS-related illness caused by HIV infection; (b) persons who are asymptomatic but exhibit serological evidence of HIV infection; and (c) persons who exhibit no evidence of HIV infection, but, due to their association with a high risk group, suffer discrimination based upon the fear of contracting AIDS.

In a discussion of employment discrimination involving persons with AIDS, Leonard asserts that the underlying premise of the Rehabilitation Act is to insure that persons with actual or perceived disabilities will not be prevented from performing activities they are fully capable of undertaking simply because of the discriminatory views that "unfairly ignore their individual qualifications and (are) based on prejudicial beliefs" regarding a particular group of individuals.[87]

Shumaker suggested that Congress astutely recognized that "the sanctions imposed by the Rehabilitation Act should depend upon the existence of a discriminatory motive in an employer's mind, and not upon the presence

---

84. Id.
85. 45 C.F.R. § 84.3. (1985).
86. Id.
87. Leonard, *Employment Discrimination Against Persons With AIDS*, 10 DAYTON L. REV. 681 (1985) at 696.

of a handicap in an employee's body.''[88] This point of view was articulated in *E. E. Black, Limited v. Marshall* when the court inferred that Congressional intent behind the Rehabilitation Act was to:

> protect people who are denied employment because of an employer's perceptions, whether or not those perceptions are accurate. It is of little solace to a person denied employment to know that the employer's view of his or her condition is erroneous. To such a person the perception of the employer is as important as reality.[89]

Based on the previous analysis, it is apparent that AIDS qualifies as a "physical or mental impairment which substantially limits one or more (of its victim's) major life activities.''[90] Because of their handicapping condition, persons with AIDS will be granted legal protection from discrimination under the Rehabilitation Act. Unfortunately, few courts have attempted to analyze the definition of "handicapped individual" as it exists in section 706(7)(B) with any significant detail. Historically, cases that have been examined under the Rehabilitation Act involve physical,[91] or mental[92] disabilities which fall easily within the statutory definition of what constitutes a handicap.

The court in *Tudyman v. United Airlines*[93] explained the lack of detail in this area of law by stating that "very few cases spend much time on the issue, as the issue usually requires little analysis.''[94] This statement fails to address the problems faced by people who are forced to endure discrimination because of AIDS. The apparent lack of precedent within case law complicates the question as to whether such individuals are indeed handicapped. Although this point may appear absurd in a case involving a fulminating AIDS victim, the problem becomes rather nettlesome when the symptoms are less apparent or even absent. There are a number of recent cases, however, that provide substantial support for the argument that AIDS is a protected handicap.

The federal court in *Black* attempted to interpret section 706 of the Rehabilitation Act for the first time since its enactment in 1973. The plain-

---

88. Shumaker, *AIDS: Does It Qualify as a Handicap Under the Rehabilitation Act of 1973*, 61 NOTRE DAME L. REV. 572 (1986), at 587.
89. 487 F. Supp. 1088 (D. Hawaii 1980) at 1097.
90. 29 U.S.C. § 706.
91. Drennon v. Philadelphia Gen. Hosp., 428 F. Supp. 809 (E.D. Pa. 1977); Simon v. St. Louis County, 656 F.2d 316 (8th Cir. 1981); Bey v. Bolger, 540 F. Supp. 910 (E.D. Pa. 1982); Norcross v. Sneed, 755 F.2d 113 (8th Cir. 1985).
92. Doe v. New York Univ., 666 F.2d 761 (2d Cir. 1981).
93. 608 F. Supp. 739 (C.D. Cal. 1984).
94. *Id.* at 744.

tiff's contention in this case hinged upon the allegation that the definition of a handicapped individual was unconstitutionally vague. After examining the legal history of the enactment, the court rejected this allegation by concluding that "Congress wanted the statute to have broad coverage and effect."[95] As part of its determination, the court also concluded that the term "impairment" meant "any condition which weakens, diminishes, restricts, or otherwise damages an individual's health or physical or mental activity."[96] Considering the morbidity that is commonly encountered by its victims, AIDS would certainly qualify as an impairment under this line of reasoning.

In analyzing the term "substantially limits," the *Black* court determined that the emphasis should be "on the individual job seeker and not solely on the impairment."[97] The court also recognized that "if an individual were disqualified from the same or similar jobs throughout the area to which he had reasonable access," his impairment would be considered to be "substantially limiting." The court quickly attached a caveat to this statement by saying that "what is to be considered a similar job must be determined on a case-by-case basis, and may differ among individuals with similar impairments, depending upon their training, education, etc."[98] Nonetheless, AIDS would still qualify as an impairment under this interpretation because it substantially limits the activity of those persons afflicted with the disorder. In addition, victims of AIDS may experience widespread discrimination because of the social paranoia that presently exists concerning AIDS. Excluding for the moment employer concerns regarding high insurance costs and employee relations, AIDS would seem to qualify as a handicap under interpretations espoused by the *Black* court.

The public health risks associated with the human immunodeficiency virus may be viewed by some as a major obstacle in the attempt to have AIDS classified as a protected handicap. Although the risk of transmission might differentiate AIDS from what has historically been recognized as "traditional" handicaps, this fact alone does not preclude it from coverage under the Rehabilitation Act. In *School Board of Nassau County v. Arline*,[99] the Eleventh Circuit Court of Appeals ruled that the contagious disease of tuberculosis does qualify as a protected handicap under the Rehabilitation Act. The case focused upon the dismissal of a Florida elementary school teacher because of her susceptibility to tuberculosis.

---

95. E. E. Black Ltd. v. Marshall, 497 F. Supp. 1088 (D. Hawaii 1980) at 1098.
96. *Id.* at 1098.
97. *Id.* at 1100.
98. *Id.* at 1101.
99. 772 F.2d 759 (11th Cir. 1985), *aff'd*, 107 S. Ct. 1123 (1987).

In its review of the law, the court found that there was no legal basis available to support the assertion that the Rehabilitation Act should protect only those persons with "traditional" handicaps. This conclusion was based, in part, on evidence that was presented concerning the opinions of HHS officials who believed that they had "no flexibility within the statutory definition to limit the term to persons who have severe, permanent, or progressive conditions that are most commonly regarded as handicaps."[100] The court concurred with this interpretation rendered by HHS officials. In its rejection of the argument that tuberculosis did not constitute a handicap within the meaning of the Rehabilitation Act, the court stated:

> Neither the regulations nor the statutory language give any indication that chronic contagious diseases are to be excluded from the definition of 'handicap'...Congress' failure to exclude contagious diseases from coverage when it specifically excluded alcoholism and drug abuse implies that it harbored no similar disapproval upon them.[101]

After it rendered its decision regarding the applicability of the Rehabilitation Act to tuberculosis, the *Arline* court turned its attention to a discussion of the term "otherwise qualified" as it applied to the particular circumstances of this case. Throughout the proceedings, the board asserted that it owed no responsibility toward accommodating the plaintiff's illness because of its overriding "duty to the public it serves" in preventing further transmission of this contagion. Referring to the board's perception of "duty," the court cited dicta from *Southeastern Community College v. Davis*,[102] stating that section 504 proscribes liability denial by public agencies that "arbitrarily deprive genuinely qualified handicapped persons of the opportunity to participate in a covered program."[103]

The *Arline* court was conscious of the fact that certain physical qualifications may be necessary for an individual to perform a particular job. The court felt, however, that it was more compelling to stress the importance of reaching a "well-informed" judgment, rather than falling prey to "reflexive reactions grounded in ignorance or capitulating to public prejudice."[104] Recognizing these important considerations, the court reversed and remanded the case for further consideration as to the plaintiff's suitability for employment in her present position, or whether

---

100. 45 C.F.R. § 84, app. A. (1985).
101. School Bd. of Nassau County v. Arline, 772 F.2d 759 (11th Cir. 1985), *aff'd*, 107 S. Ct. 1123 (1987) at 764.
102. 442 U.S. 397, 99 S. Ct. 2361, 60 L.Ed.2d 345 (1979).
103. *Id.* at 412.
104. *See also* New York State Ass'n for Retarded Children, Inc. v. Carey, 612 F.2d 644 (2d Cir.1979); Strathie v. Department of Transp., 716 F.2d 229 (3d Cir. 1983).

"reasonable accommodations" could be afforded her in some other position where the risks of infecting others would be reduced.[105] In 1986, the *Arline* decision was reviewed and subsequently upheld by the United States Supreme Court.

Although the meaning assigned to "handicapped" under the Rehabilitation Act may influence how state courts and agencies define it under their laws, states are not bound to follow the federal lead. It should be noted that the limits of legal protection afforded victims of disabling diseases under most handicap discrimination laws extends only to those individuals who are "otherwise qualified" to carry out the duties and responsibilities of their employment.[106] Under this legal interpretation, an employer is not obligated to continue the employment of an individual whose mental and/or physical condition makes reasonable job performance impossible.

Employers are required by federal law to "make reasonable accommodation" for disabled employees unless it can be shown that such accommodation "would impose an undue hardship" on the operation of the program. The determination as to whether the accommodation of an employee's disability would impose an undue hardship is based on a variety of factors including the overall size and nature of the program as well as the cost involved in accommodating the disability. It should be noted that employers "are not required to find another job for an employee who is not qualified for the job he or she was doing," but otherwise qualified employees with disabilities may not be denied "alternative employment opportunities reasonably available under employer's existing policies.[107]

Although case law on the issue of AIDS as a handicapping illness is limited, those courts that have considered the question have generally agreed with the liberal interpretation articulated by the *Black* and *Arline* courts. The law, however, generally makes exceptions for discrimination when there is a great danger to others. This is particularly true in the area of public health. Despite the present medical and scientific evidence which suggests that AIDS is not communicated through casual contact, officials at the Centers for Disease Control state that there are specific instances where greater precaution is warranted. To illustrate this point, parallels are often drawn between the human immunodeficiency virus and the hepatitis B virus. Like AIDS, hepatitis B has no known cure and can be transmitted through sexual contact, exposure to blood or blood

---

105. School Bd. of Nassau Co. v. Arline, 772 F.2d 759 (11th Cir. 1985, *aff'd*, 107 S. Ct. 1123 (1987) at 765.
106. *See* Southeastern Community College v. Davis, 442 U.S. 397, 99 S. Ct. 2361, 60 L.Ed.2d (1979) at 410.
107. Arline, *supra* note 103, n. 19 at 1131.

products, or perinatally from mother to child.[108] Because of its epidemiological similarity to HIV, the hepatitis B virus has been utilized in statistical models to predict the future course of the AIDS epidemic. Researchers at CDC believe that because the risk of acquiring hepatitis B is "far in excess" of the risk of contracting AIDS, the information that is derived from these models represents a worst case scenario for the spread of AIDS.[109] Based on this observation, CDC officials maintain that if an institution diligently follows the recommendations for preventing the spread of hepatitis B in the workplace, exposure to a person with AIDS poses no danger of infection to the healthy individual.[110]

The parallels often drawn between the hepatitis B virus and the AIDS virus have been observed within case law. In *New York State Association for the Mentally Retarded, Inc. v. Carey,*[111] a plan was devised by the New York City Board of Education to segregate certain mentally retarded children from their peers because they were known carriers of hepatitis B. The proposed plan was predicated on the belief that if these children were allowed to remain in their normal classrooms, healthy children would soon become infected with hepatitis B. The school board, however, could not provide any medical evidence that a health risk actually existed by allowing these children to remain with their peers. On this point, the court responded by stating that the "medical evidence upon which the proposal is based is sparse and fails to demonstrate any causal relationship between the classroom setting and the transmission of the virus."[112] In addition to its consideration of the medical evidence regarding hepatitis B, the court also reflected on the significant role that education plays in bringing about the socialization of handicapped children:

> A child's chance in this society is through the educational process. A major goal of the educational process is the socialization process that takes place in the regular classroom, with the resulting capability to interact in a social way with one's peers. It is therefore imperative that every child receive an education with his or her peers insofar as it is at all possible. . . . Placement of children in abnormal environments outside of peer situations imposes additional psychological and emo-

---

108. Centers for Disease Control, *Education and Foster Care of Children Infected With Human T-lymphotropic Virus Type III/Lymphadenopathy Associated Virus,* 34 MORBIDITY AND MORTALITY WEEKLY REPORT 517, 681 & 721 (1985).
109. *Id.* at 683.
110. *Id.* at 681.
111. 612 F.2d 644 (2d Cir. 1979).
112. *Id.* at 699.

tional handicaps upon children which, added to their existing handicaps causes them greater difficulties in future life.[113]

After examining the evidence, the court determined that the school board's "showing of a purely theoretical risk of spread of hepatitis B predicated upon a philosophical causation is insufficient to offset the weighty countervailing educational needs of the affected children. No substantial justification for the proposed discrimination has been demonstrated, which absence compels [the] conclusion" that segregating carriers of the disease violates section 504 of the Rehabilitation Act.[114]

The court's finding in *Carey* was based on a determination that the students involved were "handicapped" by their medical condition. Because of their epidemiological similarity, a legal analogy can be drawn between the circumstances in *Carey* and that involving HIV carriers. Under the preceding analysis, if a similar plan were implemented to segregate HIV carriers from their classmates, the emotional and legal outcomes would undoubtedly be the same.

A New York trial court in *District 27 Community School Board v. Board of Education*[115] used the reasoning developed in *Carey* to protect the right of juvenile victims of AIDS to attend public school under section 504 of the Rehabilitation Act. In this particular case, two local school boards sought an injunction against the New York Board of Education to prohibit the admission of a child with AIDS to the public school system. In holding that the exclusion of a child with AIDS would violate section 504, the court determined that AIDS does qualify as "physical impairment" as defined in the regulations promulgated under the Act.[116] The court ruled that a covered impairment included those disorders or conditions that affect the "hemic and lymphatic" systems of the body, and because AIDS is considered as a disorder affecting T-4 lymphocytes, an integral component of these two systems, a victim of AIDS is clearly handicapped by the presence of the disease. Without analyzing whether AIDS constituted a disease that "substantially limits [the] major life activities" of its victims, the court ruled that AIDS does qualify as a protected handicap. The court also held that the automatic exclusion of children with AIDS from school would violate the equal protection clause of the fourteenth amendment because the policy failed to consider children with ARC or juvenile carriers of HIV as well.[117]

---

113. *Id.* at 696.
114. *Id.* at 682.
115. 130 Misc. 2d 398, 502 N.Y.S.2d 325 (Sup. Ct. 1986).
116. *Id.* at 414.
117. *Id.* at 413.

The similarities between the hepatitis B virus and the AIDS virus proved to be an important component of the court's analysis. In deciding this case, the court relied extensively on the comments of medical and scientific experts. A number of experts in the field of epidemiology testified that the hepatitis B virus was "far more contagious" than the virus associated with AIDS.[118] The court, therefore, was unable to enjoin the Board of Education from admitting children with AIDS to the public school system.

The foregoing examination of AIDS and the Rehabilitation Act supports the conclusion that AIDS is a protected handicap within the meaning of the Act. The statutory regulations that have been promulgated under the Rehabilitation Act clearly indicate that victims of AIDS, regardless of their real or perceived clinical status, are entitled to legal protection from discrimination.[119] The legal protection that develops from the Rehabilitation Act extends to juvenile victims of AIDS as well.

The Rehabilitation Act, however, represents only one form of legal protection that is available to children with AIDS. Children with AIDS may find additional protection from discrimination under the Education for All Handicapped Children Act (EAHCA).[120] In 1982, Congress enacted EAHCA to meet the exceptional need of handicapped children and to assure that they were granted an "equal protection under the law."[121] EAHCA grants federal funds to states and, as a condition of the receipt of these funds, requires the states to provide and maintain a "policy that assures all handicapped children the right to a free appropriate public education."[122]

In addition to the creation of legal rights for handicapped children, the EAHCA maintains a strong preference for mainstreaming. States are required to establish:

> procedures to assure that to the maximum extent appropriate, handicapped children. . .are educated with children who are not handicapped, and that special classes, separate schooling, or other removal of handicapped children from the regular educational environment occurs only when the nature or severity of the handicap is such that education in regular classes. . .cannot be achieved satisfactorily.[123]

---

118. *Id.* at 415.
119. Kube, *AIDS and Employment Discrimination Under the Federal Rehabilitation Act of 1973 and Virginia's Rights of Persons With Disabilities Act*, 30 RICHMOND L. REV. 425 (1986); Titus, *AIDS as a Handicap Under the Federal Rehabilitation Act of 1973*, 43 WASH. & LEE L. REV. 1515 (1986).
120. Jones, *The Education For All Handicapped Children Act: Coverage of Children With Acquired Immune Deficiency Syndrome (AIDS)*, 15 J.L. & ED. 195 (1986).
121. 20 U.S.C. §§ 1400-1454 (1982) & Supp. III (1985).
122. *Id.* at § 1401 (18).
123. *Id.* at § 1412 (5) (B).

The application of the Education for All Handicapped Children Act to juvenile victims of AIDS is an unsettled area of the law. Like the Rehabilitation Act of 1973, EAHCA appears to include children with AIDS under certain terms. The statutory language of the EAHCA defines handicapped children as those who are "mentally retarded, hard of hearing, deaf, speech or language impaired...or other health impaired children."[124] The term "other health impaired children" is clarified further under regulations that implement the statute. In that context, the law protects those persons who suffer from "limited strength (or) vitality...due to chronic or acute health problems."[125] As noted previously, persons with AIDS suffer with a chronic health impairment that substantially interferes with their strength and vitality. The existence of this impairment would seem to be medically and legally sufficient to qualify a child for protection under the Education for All Handicapped Children Act.

The solution to the dilemma faced by children with AIDS is certainly not clear-cut. Under EAHCA mandate, these children are entitled to a free appropriate education and mainstreaming where possible. Exceptions to the mainstreaming requirement, however, have been noted in specific circumstances where the safety of other students is involved. In *Carol A. ex rel. Victoria L. v. District Board of Lee County*,[126] a Florida court found no violation when the placement of a handicapped child was changed prior to a due process hearing because the child was seen as a threat to her other classmates. Similarly in *Jackson v. Franklin City School Board*,[127] a Mississippi court ruled that the board's decision to suspend a student for sexual misconduct did not violate the provisions of the Education for All Handicapped Children Act. In its analysis of the case, the court stated that the school board owed a duty not only to the handicapped child but also to the other students within the same educational environment. In performing its duty, the school system had to strike a balance between the possible harm to the handicapped child and the potential harm to other students. The harm to the handicapped students was perceived by the court as minimal because the child had been offered additional educational services. In its decision to uphold the school board, the court reasoned that "any harm suffered by Jackson is outweighed by the defendants' showing that his presence would interfere with the providing of effective educational services to other students."[128]

---

124. *Id.* at § 1401 (a) (1).
125. 34 C.F.R. § 300.5 (b)(7), 1986.
126. 741 F.2d 369 (11th Cir. 1984); *see also*, Honig v. Doe, 484 U.S. 305, 108 S. Ct. 592, 98 L.Ed.2d 686 (1988).
127. 606 F. Supp. 152 (S.D. Miss. 1985).
128. *Id.* at 154.

The balancing approach utilized in *Jackson* is particularly applicable to the situation faced by school administrators in dealing with the question of AIDS. In attempting to strike an equitable balance between the parties involved, a difficulty arises in determining where the potential harm to other children exists. In *Carey*, the court determined that a "remote theoretical possibility" of transmitting a disease was insufficient to exclude a handicapped child from school.[129] Even when the potential risk to healthy children appears to be more compelling, courts have routinely relied on the medical community for guidance in deciding cases involving communicable diseases. In *Community High School District 155 v. Denz*,[130] an Illinois court was confronted with a case involving a student with infectious hepatitis that was excluded from public school in order to protect the health of other school children. The court ruled in favor of the infected student on the opinions of medical experts who testified that the disease was difficult to communicate.[131] In 1987, however, the testimony of medical experts was used by the court in *Martinez v. School Board of Hillsborough County*,[132] when it decided not to grant an injunction against a local school board for its refusal to enroll a child with AIDS to a trainable mentally handicapped (TMH) educational program. The court in its deliberation of the case reasoned that specific epidemiological factors relating to both the child and the AIDS virus were sufficient to justify the child's exclusion from the TMH educational program.

The issue of whether to mainstream children with AIDS hinges upon the reliability of the medical and scientific information that presently exists. Based on the medical information that is presently available on this disease, there is no reason to believe that the AIDS virus is communicated casually. Researchers at the Centers for Disease Control have stated that for the majority of children with AIDS, the benefits of attending school would be greater than the "apparent nonexistent risk of transmission" of the disease. There are notable exceptions, however, observed within the Centers for Disease Control guidelines regarding preschool children and children who lack control of their bodily secretions, who have a history of biting, or have uncoverable oozing sores which could affect the placement of children with AIDS.[133]

---

129. New York State Ass'n for the Mentally Retarded, Inc. v. Carey, 612 F.2d 644 (2d Cir. 1979).
130. 124 Ill. App. 3d 129, 463 N.E.2d 998 (Ill. App. Ct. 1984).
131. *Id.* at 129.
132. 675 F. Supp. 1574 (M.D. Fla. 1987).
133. Centers for Disease Control, *Educational and Foster Care of Children Infected With Human T-lymphotropic Virus Type III/Lymphadenopathy Associated Virus*, 34 MORBIDITY AND MORTALITY WEEKLY REPORT 517 (1985).

The National Education Association (NEA) issued a similar set of guidelines to public school officials throughout the United States.[134] According to NEA recommendations, school officials should approach the issue of AIDS on a case-by-case basis. The decision to admit or exclude children with AIDS from school should involve a group composed of the child's parents and physician, various appropriate school personnel, as well as other members of the public health community. The importance of this process was illustrated in *Board of Education v. Coopermen*[135] when the court determined that the policy guideline promulgated by the State Board of Education directing the admission of children with AIDS to regular classes did not afford local boards of education procedural due process. Utilizing medical testimony concerning children and AIDS, the court reasoned that a sufficient risk of exposure exists within the educational environment to warrant hearings prior to admission of seropositive children to regular classrooms.

The suggestions offered by the National Education Association and the Centers for Disease Control integrate well into the statutory requirements of both the Rehabilitation Act and the Education for All Handicapped Children Act. The emphasis on an individualized educational program in meeting the needs of handicapped children has become an important cornerstone of the latter Act.[136] As courts have emphasized the individualized educational plan, a blanket exclusion of a child with a certain type of disease may be a difficult position to defend legally or medically. It would not be unreasonable under the Education for All Handicapped Children Act, however, to examine the health and behavior of a child in order to determine the possible risks either to the child or to other members of the educational endeavor. If after such an analysis a real danger was determined, the existence of that danger would probably be sufficient to overrule the mainstreaming requirement of the Act. It would not, however, release the school from its duty to provide an adequate educational alternative.

Legislative Actions Concerning AIDS

The legislative history concerning AIDS is relatively short. Since 1983, there has been a flurry of legislative activity on the subject of AIDS.

---

134. National Education Association, *Recommended Guidelines For Dealing With AIDS in the Schools*, 56 J. SCHOOL HEALTH 129 (1986).
135. 507 A.2d 253 (Super. Ct. App. Div. 1986).
136. The importance of the individualized educational approach in dealing with handicapped children was affirmed by the Supreme Court in Board of Educ. of the Hendrick Hudson Cent. School Dist. v. Rowley, 458 U.S. 176 (1982).

Initially, much of the legislative action focused on public awareness and education.[137] More recently, interest in AIDS has expanded considerably. In an investigation of state legislative activity, Lewis reports that over 450 bills encompassing 34 states were introduced on the subject of AIDS in 1987 alone indicating the "serious public health concern raised by this disease in every part of the country."[138] The effects of this legislative furor are being observed within the legal community. The Council of Chief School Officials reported that of the 50 states and the District of Columbia, 28 states currently have a state policy or law on AIDS education and 24 states have mandated that AIDS education be taught in schools. The report also notes that 25 states possess a state policy regarding the attendance of students with AIDS in school.[139]

The enactment of AIDS-related legislation will have a significant impact on the development of policy in public education. Excluding AIDS educational programs, the present legislative activity concerning AIDS can be categorized under 10 major subject areas: antibody testing, blood and blood products, confidentiality, employment, housing, informed consent, insurance, marriage, prison population, and reporting.[140] Legislative actions within the categories of antibody testing, confidentiality, employment, informed consent, and reporting have significant impact upon AIDS policy formation within the public school environment.

Antibody Testing

The issue of antibody testing is fraught with social and legal pitfalls.[141] Currently, antibody testing is conducted using the enzyme-linked immunosorbent assay (ELISA) and the Western Blot tests. The degree of reliability and the safeguards necessary for each of these two tests depends on how the results are used in combating AIDS. Where the test results are applied or evaluated in aggregate and there is no impact on any one person, the ELISA alone may provide the necessary information concerning the progress of the epidemic because of its high sensitivity and specificity for the AIDS virus. In the absence of inexpensive, more reliable serological procedures, the ELISA test will continue to have an important impact

---

137. Lewis, *Acquired Immunodeficiency Syndrome: State Legislative Activity,* 258 J. AM. MED. A. 2410 (1987).
138. *Id.* at 2410.
139. Council of Chief School Officers, *AIDS Education Needs,* AIDS ED. BULL. BD. (June, 1988) at 1.
140. Lewis, *supra* note 135, at 2410.
141. *AIDS Test Examined,* ECONOMIST, July 2, 1988, at 70.

within the blood banking and research industries.[142] The complexion of the antibody testing issue changes dramatically when it has the potential to adversely affect a person through social prejudice and discrimination or when it is used as a condition precedent to compulsory health measures. In either case, the urgency for test reliability and legal safeguards becomes greater. A number of courts have broached these issues within the last few years. The prevailing legal viewpoint maintains that there is no justifiable use for antibody testing when the general benefit to be gained by the screening is outweighed by the potential for adverse social and legal consequences for an individual.

Outside of its utility in protecting the blood supply and in research, there is no convincing public health rationale for universal antibody testing. There are valid reasons for this conclusion. First, the novel biochemistry of the AIDS virus makes it difficult to detect the presence of the virus in some individuals. Second, the virus associated with AIDS exhibits a variable incubation time. Individuals would have to be subjected to periodic antibody testing to monitor adequately their status. Third, there is an unacceptably high false-positive rate associated with the ELISA test, which may be as high as twenty percent.[143] Compared to a four percent false-positive rate for the Western Blot test, the use of the ELISA test would appear to be contraindicated. Expense and technical difficulty, however, prohibit extensive use of the Western Blot test in serological examinations. Four, even if a more reliable and inexpensive test could be developed, compulsory antibody testing would undoubtedly have a significant impact on society. Beyond the inherent legal complications, compulsory antibody testing would alienate many of the same people that testing was originally intended to help by making them reluctant to seek out competent medical assistance. Extensive compulsory serological testing would also reduce public compliance with voluntary health measures. Five, universal serological testing would not be economically or technically feasible considering the sheer numbers of people involved in the process. Although this disadvantage may not apply to small populations, there remains no compelling legal justification for disparate blood testing in light of the scientific and epidemiological evidence presently available on AIDS.

In spite of these observations, 13 state legislatures have acted on the issue of antibody testing.[144] Most of this legislation centers on the establish-

---

142. Sarngadharan, Popovic, Bruch, Schupach, and Gallo, *Antibodies Reactive With Human T-lymphotropic Retroviruses (HTLV-III) in the Serum of Patients With AIDS*, 224 Sci. 506 (1984).

143. Schoors, Berkowitz, Cumming, Katz, and Sandler, *Prevalence of HIV Antibody in American Blood Donors*, 313 New Eng. J. Med. 384 (1985).

144. Lewis, *supra* note 135, at 2410.

ment of testing sites and procedural requirements. Some states have enacted very specific laws concerning HIV antibody testing. In Colorado and Iowa, for example, public health officials have been granted the authority to subject suspected communicable disease carriers to involuntary physical and serological examinations. Under a similar Florida enactment, all convicted prostitutes are required to undergo serological testing for sexually transmitted diseases, including HIV.[145]

Confidentiality

While victims of AIDS recognize the critical role that scientific research plays in the effort to understand, treat, and prevent this disease, they are concerned that the disclosure of research information may prove detrimental to their interests. Historically, the interaction observed between the public and scientific community has been dependent upon the level of confidence that exists within the general population. Interaction between the public and scientific community increases when people are confident that a system exists to protect their rights and that people with whom they will be working are competent and trustworthy.[146] In light of this observation, the following guideline is suggested:

> No individual, organization or agency should have access to any personally identifiable information gathered in research or surveillance on AIDS for any other purpose other than AIDS research or surveillance without the consent of the individuals or subjects.[147]

The issue of confidentiality is compelling indeed. As the incidence of AIDS continues to expand into the public school environment, an increasing number of educational personnel will have to deal with the tension between the duty to disclose pertinent medical information concerning AIDS to protect other members of society[148] and the responsibility to safeguard the confidentiality of personal medical information.[149] This

---

145. Centers for Disease Control, *Antibody to Human Immunodeficiency Virus in Female Prostitutes*, 36 MORBIDITY AND MORTALITY WEEKLY REPORT 157 (1987).
146. Bayer, Levine, and Murray, *Guidelines For Confidentiality in Research on AIDS* 72, in AIDS AND PATIENT MANAGEMENT: LEGAL, ETHICAL AND SOCIAL ISSUES (M. D. Witt ed. 1986).
147. *Id.* at 77.
148. *See* McIntosh v. Milano, 403 A.2d 500 (Super Ct. App. Div. 1979); Tarashoff v. Regents of the Univ. of Cal., 17 Cal. 3d 425, 551 P.2d 334, 131 Cal. Rptr. 14 (1976).
149. *See* South Fla. Blood Serv. Inc. v. Rasmussen, 467 So. 2d 798 (Fla. Dist. Ct. App. 1985); Farnsworth v. Procter and Gamble Co., 758 F.2d 1545 (11th Cir. 1985); District 27 Community School Bd. v. Board of Educ., 130 Misc. 2d 398, 502 N.Y.S.2d 325 (Sup. Ct. 1986).

is a vitally important matter for all public school employees who teach, interact, supervise or care for AIDS victims.[150] In the final analysis, the impact of the AIDS epidemic on the educational environment will depend on the balance that is struck between these two opposing interests.[151]

The issue of confidentiality has become so important that researchers at George Washington University report that many states have attempted to strengthen the confidentiality of medical, public health, and scientific records by reviewing procedures presently used to ensure the confidentiality of records and by amending existing or drafting new legislation that focuses specifically on matters associated with confidentiality.[152] Although no true guarantee of confidentiality may ever exist, the fact that many states are considering the problem increases the probability that future victims of handicapping illnesses, such as AIDS, will be able to avoid the discrimination and social prejudice that often results when personal medical information is indiscriminately disclosed to the public.

Seventeen states have enacted laws to establish the confidentiality of research and medical information. Of those, only four states have passed laws to require written informed consent of a person before permitting any serological examinations for the AIDS viral antibody.[153] Legislative activity in the areas of confidentiality and informed consent will undoubtedly increase in the future considering the communicability of the AIDS virus and the urgency for reliable scientific information.

Discrimination

Sixteen states have enacted laws directly prohibiting either AIDS-based discrimination or the use of serum tests to screen employees for AIDS or HIV infection.[154] A San Francisco public interest law firm, the National Gay Rights Advocates, reported that approximately 24 states have indicated that they will interpret and extend their present legislation prohibiting discrimination against the handicapped to apply to victims of AIDS. It is also projected that at least 10 of these same states will extend their

---

150. *See* Fleming and Maximov, *The Patient or His Victim: The Therapist's Dilemma*, 62 CAL. L. REV. 1025 (1974); George, Korin, Quattrone and Mandel, *The Therapist's Duty to Protect Third Parties: A guide for the Perplexed*, 14 RUTGERS L. J. 637 (1983); Roth and Meisel, *Dangerousness, Confidentiality, and the Duty to Warn*, 134 AM. J. PSYCH 508 (1977).
151. Anderson, *AIDS-Related Litigation: The Competing Interests Surrounding Discovery of Blood Donors' Identities*, 19 IND. L. REV. 561 (1986).
152. Intergovernmental Health Policy Project, *A Summary of AIDS Law From the 1986 Legislative Sessions*, GEO. WASH. UNIV. (1987) at 25.
153. Lewis, *supra* note 135, at 2412.
154. *Id.*

legislative protection against discrimination to persons with ARC and HIV infection. Laws governing unemployment, health, and pension benefits may also afford some protection as well as provide some relief to the victims of AIDS.[155]

Some states have adopted a wait-and-see attitude with respect to the problem of AIDS discrimination. This stance could prove to be a major obstacle to the successful implementation of public health strategies necessary to constrain the future course of the AIDS epidemic. It is quite unlikely that individuals at high risk for AIDS will come forward for testing and counseling or seek medical treatment if they perceive that some form of discrimination may follow.[156]

Summary

The legal debate regarding the placement of AIDS-linked children within the educational milieu will likely continue well into the future. As additional scientific evidence contributes to the understanding of the disease, questions now present may be answered. School officials must not become complacent, however. Questions concerning the admission or placement of children with AIDS in public school should be examined on an individual basis. Although prevailing medical evidence suggests that there is little risk of contagion, reasonable people can conclude that even a minimal risk is too great when a human life is involved. The emotional reactions brought about by this dilemma will continue to fuel the fires of concern that exist throughout the United States. School officials must seek to balance various competing interests if they are to deal effectively with students and employees with AIDS. Based on the present scientific and legal information concerning AIDS, a comprehensive policy of excluding victims of the disease from public school would not seem justified. The more prudent course would be to utilize the legal precedent establish in *Jackson* to examine each circumstance on an individual basis in light of reliable legal and medical advice as to how this balance can be obtained equitably. Only in this way can school officials prevent the possibility of a misinformed majority from forcing its wishes upon an innocent minority.

---

155. Leonard, *AIDS in the Workplace* 106 in AIDS AND THE LAW: A GUIDE FOR THE PUBLIC (H.L. Dalton and S. Burris eds 1987).
156. Brandt, *AIDS in Historical Perspective* 37 in AIDS AND THE LAW: A GUIDE FOR THE PUBLIC (H.L. Dalton and S. Burris eds. 1987).

CHAPTER IV
THE FORMATION OF EDUCATIONAL POLICY

Introduction

The process of policy formation within the public school environment hinges upon the ability of administrators to balance the interaction that exists among various interests groups. The task of policy formation within public schools has become more difficult since AIDS was identified in 1981. The complex and emotional features of the AIDS epidemic have created an explosive environment within which an effective policy response must be developed by the educational community. The explosive nature of the AIDS crises has made many school policy officials feel as if they have been locked in a dark, gas-filled room with a book of matches.

Despite the explosive nature of the educational environment, many school administrators have struggled to formulate policies that would protect the rights of the few children who were ill as well as the vast majority who were healthy. Unfortunately, the task has been extremely difficult, and many public school administrators have found that they have neither the experience nor the expertise to cope with the present circumstance. Like many other public officials, educational administrators find themselves in the midst of a policy dilemma for which no model or paradigm exists. In the absence of an appropriate communicable disease model, many officials have attempted to utilize models involving polio or hepatitis to formulate new policy. Unfortunately, each of these approaches has exemplified a certain degree of inadequacy in dealing with the present task of formulating an effective public school policy concerning AIDS.

This chapter discusses the development of policy as it occurs within the organizational environment. The first part of the chapter discusses a variety of factors that have influenced the development of public policy in this country. The second part of the chapter focuses on public school policy development specifically. Using information from previous chapters, various scientific, legal, and social factors associated with AIDS are discussed within the context of public school policy development.

An Overview of Public Policy Formation

The process of policy formation is a fundamental component of institutional and organizational existence. Policy formation is necessary for the allocation of resources and in defining the priorities necessary to guide official actions.[1] Within industrial and developing societies where increasing complexity, rapid change, and continuous tension are concomitant with social existence, the exigency for policy formation is more compelling. The process of policy formation involves a conscious effort to make value choices in order to set priorities and to commit economic resources.[2] The incidence of acquired immunodeficiency syndrome has complicated the process of policy formation within the public health field. Despite the efforts of many individuals within the scientific and medical communities to control AIDS, the pandemic continues its unwavering attack on society. Coupled with the fact that currently no appropriate policy model exists to respond to any major health problem in the United States, AIDS poses an incomparable challenge to those public officials seeking to restrain its future progression.

In the effort to formulate public policy, there is a subtle tendency to confuse policy formation with decision making within the organization environment. Although these two concepts are not mutually exclusive, differences exist between them. A decision reflects "the reduction of alternatives to a single move and the prediction of a particular set of consequences."[3] Decisions are primarily concerned with present action and the data and methodologies requisite for immediate response. In contrast, the concept of policy "presumes the construction of possible and plausible alternatives and their general consequences and their evaluation in terms of normative criteria, rather than merely the calculation or assessment of functional efficiency".[4] Policy may be regarded as an indication of intention or a guide to action. Policy encompasses values which establish social priorities in relations between government and society. Policy decisions are "specific events reflecting a confluence of values and behavior which guide administrative action and may be expressed in legislation, judicial decisions, executive orders, or administrative rules and regulations."[5]

There is no question that policy plays a significant role in the decision-making process. There is a danger, however, that policy formulation may be construed as nothing more than the formation of a rule for the purpose of making more than one immediate decision. This interpretation incorrectly assumes that the process of policy formation merely represents an extension of the process by which one arrives at a single decision. Policy

---

1. C. E. LINDBLOM, THE POLICY-MAKING PROCESS (1968).
2. C. P. CHELF, PUBLIC POLICYMAKING IN AMERICA (1981); see also Harmon, Administration Policy Formulation and the Public Interest, 29 PUB. ADMIN. REV. 483 (Sept., 1969).
3. Johnson Jr., Educational Policy Study and the Historical Perspective, 11 ED. ADMIN. QUART. 40 (1975).
4. Id. at 40.
5. Simmons, Davis, Chapman and Sager, Policy Flow Analysis: A Conceptual Model for Comparative Public Policy Research, 27 W. POL'Y. Q. 461 (1974).

formation is a "systematic attempt to shape the future" rather than a set of random or tactical responses designed merely to satisfy a particular end or commitment.[6]

Policy formation is also a dynamic process involving the interaction of various interest groups. The process of policy formation depends upon the changing nature of modern society.[7] The conceptual basis for this view of policy formation is more easily understood if approached as networks of processes involving the interaction of various subsystems that collide intermittently or continuously within the political system. Within this heuristic, a subsystem may encompass the executive, legislative, or judicial branches of government, independent agencies, special interest groups, individuals, or the mass impact of the larger community.

Policy formation is dependent upon the vitality of these political processes which function in blending the power and value of colliding subsystems. Although every subsystem can participate in the policy making process, each is constrained by formal and informal arrangements that are derived from the total political system. These arrangements ultimately determine which policy choices are to be made by the system. The process of public policy formation can be defined as:

> A sequential flow of interactions between government and nongovernment participants who discuss, argue about, and find common grounds for agreeing on the scope and types of governmental actions in dealing with a particular societal problem [8]

The milieu of such policy formation is best described as dynamic, in that it grows, changes, and develops to meet various societal priorities, needs, or wants. Policy formation is contingent upon the mobilization of energy and resources by specific groups and individuals. These requirements make it extremely difficult for individuals or small groups to participate in the political process of policy formation. When individuals or groups become integrated into the process as subsystems, they aggressively pursue their own interests through policy decisions. Over time, the actors or groups within a particular subsystem may develop a particular style which influences their activity and interest toward certain policy decisions. This distinctive style reflects an historical perspective that restricts and refines their actions and concerns. The effect of this process has become a salient feature of both political parties in the United States.

---

6. Rothwell, *Forward* to THE POLICY SCIENCES: RECENT DEVELOPMENTS IN SCOPE AND METHOD at ix (D. Lerner and H. D. Lasswell eds. 1951).
7. T.R DYE, UNDERSTANDING PUBLIC POLICY (1984).
8. Lyden, Shipman and Wilkinson, *Decision Flow Analysis: A Methodology for Studying the Policy Making Process*, in P. LE BRETON, COMPARATIVE ADMINISTRATIVE THEORY 155 (1968).

Beyond the effects of the subsystems themselves, there are numerous variables within the environment that contribute to the dynamics observed within the policy formation process. These variables evolve from inter-societal changes, technological developments, generational dialectics, and resource availability.[9] The unanticipated consequences of earlier policy decisions may also impact the policy process as extrasystemic inputs because they provide an impetus for change. These unanticipated consequences of prior policy decisions are never completely revealed to all of the participants within the process and are rarely assessed rationally. The process of policy formation exhibits varying tendencies toward equilibrium, hypertrophy, and entropy when viewed as a system.[10] Institutional systems, like their biological counterparts, will experience a greater movement toward entropy or disorder when the supply of energy and resources becomes scarce. Without the requisite energy or resources, the system will expend its own reserves to maintain its existence. Ultimately the system fails and policy formation ceases. A system exhibits hypertrophy when one characteristic or subsystem has become so dominant that change becomes arduous or impossible. In this dysfunctional state, the social need that initiated the process no longer is served and policy formation abates. In comparison to the dysfunctional effects of either entropy or hypertrophy, equilibrating tendencies contribute to the survival of participating actors and groups, as well as to the continuation of their specific policy concerns.

Policy formation "is not properly analogous to the processes of description and calculation that are inherent to decision making, but to the process of human choice as a rational, value-oriented enterprise."[11] This definition of policy formation hinges upon three crucial characteristics. First, the process of policy formation is inextricably bound to the construction and subsequent acceptance of normative criteria that influence both the analysis and construction of policy. Second, the strategic nature of policy formation assumes that policy functions over extended periods of time. Although previous policy can be analyzed descriptively, the process of policy formation requires a different intellectual process as well as a different mode of specification. Third, the study and formulation of policy lies in the effort to maximize potential goals and alternative courses of action and the weighing of them in terms of warranted principles of value.[12] Over time, this process has become known as a cost-benefit analysis.

---

9. Simmons, Davis, Chapman and Sager, *supra* note 5, at 459. The authors define these variables as "extrasystemic inputs."
10. D. EASTON, A FRAMEWORK FOR POLITICAL ANALYSIS (1965).
11. Johnson, *supra* note 3, at 43.
12. *Id.* at 41.

The dynamic nature of the political system requires that government officials and school administrators adopt a systemic view of the entire process in order to unravel some of the complexity that exists within the policy formation environment. The inherent complexity of the policy making process can be described in an analysis of decision flow:

> Although the realistic working assumption is that a public decision is an amalgam of a variety of contributions - public attitudes amongst them - fed into a network of social interactions, the interaction path rarely shows a constant, unchanging structure; instead, it develops, evolves, and changes shape and form over time. One of the primary reasons why the public policy process has always appeared to be such a mystery to many people is this fluidity, this refusal to remain within the confines of institutional structures designed to deal with public issues.[13]

Policy research has eliminated much of the transcendental quality of public policy formation through the use of analytical tools which calibrate the network of social interactions that occur within the political system. The objective of policy research is to focus on the collective of decisions which form a public policy and bring them into perspective, rather than to center on decision paths alone. Although the task has been difficult, the goal remains attainable despite the inherent complexities of the methodologies employed.

Particularly within the last thirty years, government officials and policy administrators have relied on a variety of paradigms to formulate public policy. In an examination of public policy, Dror noted and analyzed six dissimilar policy development models: pure-rationality, economically-rational, extra-rational, sequential decision, satisfying and incremental change.[14] When an appropriate model was unavailable, many policy framers focused upon organizational goals, the political or economic environment, bureaucratic procedures, or the nature of the budget making process in their efforts to design appropriate policy. Unfortunately, many of these approaches suffer from a kind of policy myopia that makes them unsuited to the policy demand created by the AIDS crisis. If public officials are to address the issues associated with this pandemic in an effective manner, they must view the entire policy development landscape. Narrow viewpoints and myopic policy approaches will not produce the action necessary to control the AIDS epidemic nor will deal productively with its victims.

---

13. Lyden, Shipman and Wilkinson, *supra* note 8, at 156.
14. V. DROR, PUBLIC POLICY REEXAMINED (1969), at 129.

The processes that occur within the educational environment with respect to policy development are analogous to those that operate generally within the political environment. The educational environment, however, does not possess the same degree of institutional momentum that has become an obvious feature of the political world during the last century. Although there are other factors involved, size and population are two major determinants of institutional momentum. Large institutions, like large objects, tend to move ahead with very little variation in their path. Therefore, the process of policy development within large institutions is affected to a lesser degree by the activity of various subsystems as compared to policy development within small institutions.

The size and population of the political and educational institutions differ markedly from each other. The conservation effects of institutional momentum occur less within the educational endeavor than in the political enterprise because of the smaller size of the latter. As a result, policy development within the educational institution tends to change direction more frequently depending upon which subsystem has acquired the greatest power.

The responses of decision makers regarding major unresolved policy issues, such as equalizing school finance arrangements, desegregating schools, and shrinking enrollments, are likely to be "influenced more by society-wide demographic and economic conditions than by either the substance of the issue itself or the initiatives of educators."[15] Today's educators, unlike those of the 1960's, will not have the opportunity to shape the prevailing social forces that exist within the political environment to their own advantage.[16] Many of the social forces, such as school finance equalization, back-to-basics, and competency testing, that were directed at improving public education during the last 25 years have either been attenuated or redirected within the political environment.

Economic changes within the United States have also had a dramatic impact upon public education during the last 25 years. During that period of time, the United States lost its financial independence and became a debtor nation within the world economic market. With a national deficit in the trillions of dollars and the nation experiencing double digit inflation followed by mounting recession, the federal government found itself in a financial crisis. The budget was strained continuously by drives to provide additional funding for social services and national defense. The government continued its financial support of programs that focused on

---

15. Guthrie, *Emerging Politics of Educational Policy*, 3 ED. EVAL. & POL. ANAL. 75 (1981) *and see* CRITICAL ISSUES IN EDUCATIONAL POLICY: AN ADMINISTRATOR'S OVERVIEW (L. Rubin ed. 1980).
16. H. J. AARON, POLITICS AND THE PROFESSORS: THE GREAT SOCIETY PERSPECTIVE (1978).

the educational needs of exceptional or disadvantaged students, however. To minimize some of its economic burden, the federal government shifted the financial burden of many social programs to the states. As a result of this shift, the competition for state dollars has become intense, and it has often been difficult for education to obtain its share of economic and human resources.

Education in the last 60 years has progressively moved toward political and administrative centralization that has shifted "the flow of decision-making discretion to fewer persons and to more remote and higher levels of government."[17] The trend toward centralization has had a significant impact on educational policy formation at the district level. The relative inability of public school officials to make important decisions concerning district policy may further erode the base of political support for education that exists locally within the community. As the local electorate becomes more disenfranchised by the trend toward centralization, democratic initiatives, like tuition tax credits and educational vouchers, become politically more feasible.[18]

The subtle movement toward administrative and political centralization has continued unabated despite efforts to promote educational reform. Community control, alternative schools, and parents advisory council movements of the 1960's and 1970's did little to redress the imbalance of decision making authority that has existed for over 25 years. Professional officials and politically distant state and federal government officials continue to maintain a significant proportion of the decision making authority with respect to public education.

The movement toward centralization may provide additional opportunities for special interest groups to influence state and federal officials. Because centralization tends to concentrate decision making authority in a smaller number of people, this smaller population makes it easier for special interest groups to concentrate their political efforts on only those people and on issues they deem important. This kind of political activity may "increasingly alienate voters, contribute to efforts to circumvent the legislative process, and further, politicize education decisions."[19]

The maladies that plague American education today, such as demography, economics, centralization, and politicization, are exacerbated further by the AIDS crisis. The issues associated with AIDS have widened the schism that already exists between parents and local school districts concerning educational policy development. The task of policy

17. Guthrie, *supra* note 15, at 78.
18. *Id*. at 78.
19. *Id*. at 79.

development in response to AIDS is made more arduous by an absence of appropriate policy models or paradigms. Public officials and school administrators will have to integrate specific components of previous policy models and techniques into an efficacious educational policy paradigm. The process of educational policy development must reflect an awareness of historical precedent. History points to legal, scientific, and sociological variables that influence public response to epidemic disease. Those factors require attention in the process of policy formation.

The Evolution of Public Policy as Applied to Public Schools and Communicable Diseases

The Impact of State Police Power

The jurisprudence associated with government reaction to communicable disease is both complicated and uncertain. The majority of legal challenges to communicable disease policy in this country occurred during the early part of the twentieth century. The major impetus behind many of these early cases was the overriding concern exemplified by the government in protecting the general health and welfare of the nation's citizens. As the legal system grew and matured, public health law evolved in response to advancements in the fields of science and medicine. Part of the process may be attributed to a shift in political interests that enabled individual members of society to enjoy greater constitutional protection. The effects of the shift are still being observed today, and many of the concepts that emerged during that tumultuous period of legal history have yet to crystallize completely.

Throughout the history of this country, states have maintained a significant role in the promotion and maintenance of public health. The authority to regulate public health is one of the implied powers that has been granted to the states under the provisions of the tenth amendment to the United States Constitution. Although the existence of state police power has ostensibly been accepted by the general population without significant debate, it is the exercise of this power that has simulated the most discussion within the legal community. Many of the legal discussions that have occurred in the field of community health have centered on the impact of police power upon personal freedoms. In those instances where the effect of police power has been perceived as an abridgement of constitutional liberty, the judiciary has often been faced with the dilemma of balancing two opposing legal viewpoints. Courts have attempted to evaluate the merits of a disputed state action of the basis of its propriety, utility, and necessity with respect to the intended outcome.[20] Historically, as many of the constitutional issues associated with the exercise of state police power began to coalesce, the judiciary evolved a number of analytical tests that would eventually establish the criteria upon which a case in this area of law would be adjudicated.

The hallmark of many of the early cases is the latitude that was consistently afforded to the state legislatures by the courts. In many instances, state actions were presumed to be valid because of the compelling nature of the public interest involved. In this context, personal rights were often considered to be subordinate to the interests of the state. Even in those circumstances where personal freedom was severely attenuated by a particular legislative action, courts were averse to making determinations that would substitute their own judgement for that of the legislature.

The preferential treatment that was often exhibited by the courts in dealing with policy issues that were associated with public health regulation was predicated upon the belief that "a community has the right to protect itself against an epidemic disease which threatens the safety of its members."[21] This form of community self-preservation required state legislatures to enact a variety of public health measure that were aimed at reducing the incidence of epidemic disease. The focus of many of those measures was on compulsory examination and treatment, reporting and registering, immunization, disinfection, and quarantine. Although the efficacy of some of those control measures is suspect today, the legality of their existence was generally supported under the minimum scrutiny of the rational basis test if it could be demonstrated that there was a "real or substantial" relationship between the statute and its desired outcome. This presumption of validity would prevail unless it could be established that the state acted in "an arbitrary, unreasonable manner" or went "beyond what was reasonably required for the safety of the public."[22]

The Impact of Public Opinion and the Need for Rationality

The development of the rational basis test proved to be a significant event in the evolution of public policy in this country. Despite this fact, there have been numerous problems associated with its usage as a legal benchmark within the area of public health. Initially, it was difficult to decipher how "rationality" was to be judged when employing the test. In practice, the rationality of a public health measure was often seen in terms

---

20. L. TRIBE, AMERICAN CONSTITUTIONAL LAW (1978).
21. Jacobson v. Massachusetts, 197 U.S. 11, 24 Sup. Ct. 358, 49 L.Ed. 643 (1905) at 11.
22. Parmet, *AIDS and Quarantine: The Revival of an Archaic Doctrine*, 14 HOFSTRA L. REV. 76 (1985).

of whether it was necessary for preservation of public health. Unfortunately, this raised an even more basic concern regarding the criteria that would be employed by the legal community to determine necessity. Initially, the necessity of many public health measure was substantiated on the basis of what the legislature or general public thought was important in disease prevention. The effect of public opinion on the resolution of public health issues is clearly observed in *Viemeister v. White* when the court concluded:

> While we do not decide, and cannot decide, that vaccination is a preventative of smallpox, we take judicial note of the fact that this is the common belief of the people of the State, and with this fact as a foundation, we hold that the statute in question is a health law enacted in a reasonable and proper exercise of the police power.[23]

The relative impact of public opinion upon the validity of state health regulation is observed again in *State v. Rackowski* where a Connecticut court supported a public health measure aimed at controlling the transmission of scarlet fever on the basis of "common knowledge" that an exposed individual may communicate the disease to others.[24]

Although it is perhaps one of the highest goals of law to protect the personal rights of individuals, victims of communicable disease have traditionally been excluded from this protection. Systematic efforts to rectify this situation have resulted in the development of numerous validity tests that focus upon the relationship between the law and its effects on individuals. Initially, the rational basis test was seen as a viable method to clarify this relationship. Unfortunately, the test's reliance on nonscientific criteria had a deleterious effect on the personal rights of those persons the test was originally designed to protect.[25]

In the absence of scientific criteria, "suspect conduct and association" were often construed by many courts as justification for the regulation of public health. This was the circumstance in *Ex parte Company* when the Ohio Supreme Court validated a state health regulation that allowed public health officials to quarantine prostitutes and their associates on the suspicion that they were carriers of venereal disease.[26] The intrusive effects of spurious factors on private interests are also apparent in *People v. Strautz* where an Illinois court validated a state statute that allowed

---

23. 179 N.Y. 235, 72 N.E. 97 (1904) at 235.
24. 86 A. 606 (Conn. 1913).
25. *See* Kirk v. Wyman, 65 S.E. 387, 83 S. Ct. 372 (1909).
26. *Ex parte* Company, 106 Ohio Sup. Ct. 50, 139 N.E. 204 (1922); Wragg v. Griffin, 185 Iowa 243, 170 N.W. 400 (1919).

public health officials to subject "suspected" prostitutes to "a physical examination of their persons."[27]

In spite of the prevailing effects of public opinion on the disposition of these early cases, the evolution of public policy was punctuated by efforts to introduce more objective criteria into the resolution of legal conflicts involving health regulation. As early as 1896, a New York court recognized the importance of obtaining sound medical evidence prior to the imposition of control measure by stating that "the mere possibility that persons might have been exposed to such a disease (smallpox) is not sufficient." They must, in fact, have been exposed to it, the conditions must "actually exist for a communication of the contagion," and all such issues must be determined by "medical science and skill, (not) common knowledge."[28]

In perhaps one of the most significant cases of the time, a federal district court struck down a municipal quarantine order for bubonic plague involving some 15,000 Chinese inhabitants of San Francisco.[29] The court overturned the municipal ordinance on the basis of a few inconsistencies existing in the testimony offered. First, there was little evidence to indicate that bubonic plague constituted a substantial health threat to the community. Second, realizing that bubonic plague is more efficiently communicated within areas of poor sanitation and overcrowding, the utilization of a quarantine would increase the potential for transmission. Third, because the quarantine order was instituted in a predominately Chinese district of the city, there was some indication that the action may have been racially motivated. The apparent scrutiny utilized by the court in its deliberation is significant considering the scientific and medical inadequacies that existed at the beginning of the century.

Some 25 years after *Smith* was decided, a California court in *Ex parte Shepard* rejected the proposition that "mere suspicion" of venereal infection is sufficient to uphold a quarantine order given by public health officials.[30] In the same year, another California court in *Ex parte Arata* demonstrated considerable interest in protecting the constitutional rights of suspected disease carriers. According to this court, "mere suspicion" unsupported by facts giving rise to reasonable or probable cause will afford no justification at all for depriving persons of their liberty.[31]

The demand for more reliable data in the determination of necessity continued in 1923 when an Illinois court reviewed a case involving the

---

27. People v. Strautz, 386 Ill. 360, 54 N.E.2d 441 (1944) at 444.
28. Smith v. Emery, 42 N.Y.S. 258, 11 App. Div. 10 (1896) at 260.
29. Jew Ho v. Williamson, 103 F. 10 (C.C.D. Cal. 1900).
30. 52 Cal. App. 49, 139 N.E. 204 (1922) at 49.
31. 52 Cal. App. 380, 198 P. 814 (1921) at 816.

forced isolation of a healthy woman who was identified by public health officials as a carrier of typhoid fever.[32] Although the action against the woman was upheld in this case, the court articulated some important limitations on the use of police power by stressing:

> While courts will not pass on the wisdom of the means adopted to restrict and suppress the spread of contagious and infectious diseases, they will interfere if the regulations are arbitrary and unreasonable. . . . Where danger of an epidemic actually exists, health and quarantine regulations will always be sustained by the courts; but, the health regulation are sustained on the law of necessity, and when the necessity ceases, the right to enforce the regulation ceases.[33]

The Impact of Federal Legislation

The evolution of public policy in this country changed substantially soon after the Civil War when Congress enacted the fourteenth amendment. Modern courts have been more cognizant of individual rights and the importance of protecting those rights from arbitrary or irrational delimitation. With the advent of modern technology and more objective scientific criteria, courts have been diligent in requiring substantial justification for any personal control measure that is aimed at reducing the spread of epidemic disease. This fact is demonstrated in *New York State Association for Retarded Children, Inc. v. Carey* when the U. S. Court of Appeals determined that mentally retarded children who were carriers of serum hepatitis could not be excluded from attending regular school classes with their peers. In weighing the magnitude of the evidence presented, the court determined that a "remote possibility" of disease transmission was not sufficient grounds to justify the action considering "the detrimental effects of isolating the carrier children."[34] In choosing to allow carriers of serum hepatitis to attend public school unfettered by legal restraints, the court demonstrated an acute awareness of the difficulties that afflicted members of society face every day of their lives.

A similar critical view of public health necessity was undertaken in *School Board of Nassau County v. Arline* when the Florida Court of Appeals held that victims of contagious diseases are "handicapped individuals" within the meaning of section 504 of the Rehabilitation Act of 1973. In scrutinizing the evidence, the court found it appropriate to determine "whether the defendant's justifications reflect a well informed

---

32. People *ex rel.* Barmore v. Robertson, 302 Ill. 422, 134 N.E. 815 (1922).
33. *Id.* at 819 (citations omitted).
34. New York State Ass'n for the Mentally Retarded, Inc. v. Carey, 612 F.2d 644 (2d Cir. 1979).

judgment. . .or whether they are simply conclusionary statements used to justify reflexive actions grounded in ignorance or capitulation to public prejudice."[35] The relative impact of this decision was augmented substantially in 1987 when the Supreme Court reviewed *Arline*, and by a majority vote determined that section 504 does indeed protect persons with contagious diseases from discrimination. In writing for the majority, Justice Brennan emphasized that the congressional intention behind the enactment of the law was "to ensure that handicapped individuals are not denied access to jobs or other benefits because of the prejudiced attitudes or the ignorance of others."[36] The majority also recognized that the myths and fears about disability or disease are as handicapping as the physical limitations that arise from the actual impairment.

With a similar analysis, the New York court in *District 27 Community School Board v. the Board of Education* ruled that a child with acquired immunodeficiency syndrome may not be automatically excluded from public school.[37] In reviewing the evidence, the court determined that the apparent nonexistent risk of transmission of HIV in the school setting was strongly supported by a five year accumulation of epidemiological data on the disease. The automatic exclusion of children with AIDS, therefore, serves no rational purpose because it has no adequate connection with public health, safety, or welfare.[38] In presenting its conclusions, the court reiterated the importance of acquiring reliable scientific information for the formulation of health-related public policy.

The Impact of Emerging Constitutional Rights

The exigency for more objective criteria in the analysis of public health necessity was an important force in the overall development of public policy In this country. There were other forces at work, however. While efforts were being made to require more objective standards in the analysis of public health legislation, the Supreme Court was attempting to substantiate the existence of new personal freedoms.[39] In the process, the Court recognized that the rational basis test with its one dimensional approach would not provide the analysis necessary to balance the complex judicial issues that were involved in the emergence of a new constitutional standard. To rectify the problem, the Court created a multidimensional

---

35. School Bd. of Nassau County v. Arline, 772 F.2d 759 (11th Cir. 1985), *aff'd*, 107 S. Ct. 1123 (1987).
36. *Id.* at 136.
37. 130 Misc. 2d 398, 502 N.Y.S.2d 325, (Sup. Ct. 1986).
38. *Id.* at 413.
39. *See* Griswold v. Connecticut, 381 U.S. 479, 85 Sup. Ct. 1678, 14 L.Ed.2d 510 (1965); Eisenstadt v. Baird, 405 U.S. 438 (1972); Roe v. Wade, 410 U.S. 113, 93 S. Ct. 705, 35 L.Ed.2d 147 (1973).

approach with three distinct standards of review, minimum, intermediate, and strict scrutiny. The level of scrutiny that was selected by the Court depended on the nature of the righted infringed upon or the groups affected by the challenged measure.

Most cases within the field of public policy were subjected to the superficial scrutiny of the rational basis test. This fact can be partially explained by the presence of two significant sociopolitical factors. First, the initial development of public policy concerning social health was hampered by a communications gap that existed between the fields of science and law. The exchange of information across this gap was dependent on the perceived accuracy of the information, the time necessary to transfer the information, and the frequency of information exchange. Although this gap exists today, technological changes within the telecommunications field have minimized its impact. Second, the use of scientific information in the deliberation of public health litigation has historically been hampered by a cultural conflict existing between members of the medical and legal communities. In an examination of this cultural phenomenon, Fox speculated that the existence of this conflict is supported by a fundamental disagreement between lawyers and physicians concerning five issues: "the nature of authority, how conflict should be resolved, the relative importance of procedure and substance, the nature and significance of risk, and the legitimacy of politics as a method of solving problems."[40] The exigencies of the AIDS crises will undoubtedly exacerbate this situation further making it extremely difficult for lawyers and physicians to work together on issues related to the preservation of life and liberty. The existence of these sociopolitical factors has allowed the balance of interests to remain of the side of the state.[41]

Many of the conceptual problems that were associated with the rational basis test have been rectified by the development of the intermediate and strict scrutiny rests. Unfortunately, these two tests have created problems of their own within the legal community. Tribe reported that one of the major problems associated with a three tier review approach is that selection of the approach substantially influences the outcome of the case.[42] He continued his critique by arguing that virtually no legal measure has survived the analytical rigor of the strict scrutiny test and none has been overturned for lack of a rational relationship.

The apparent relationship between the standard of review employed and the judicial outcome has fostered the idea that perhaps the court is

---

40. Fox, *Physicians Versus Lawyers: A Conflict of Cultures*, in AIDS AND THE LAW, A GUIDE FOR THE PUBLIC 210 (H. L. Dalton and S. Burris eds. 1987) at 212.

41. *See* City of New Orleans v. Dukes, 427 U.S. 297 (1976).

42. L. TRIBE, AMERICAN CONSTITUTIONAL LAW sections 16-2 & 16-6 (1978).

selecting the several of scrutiny to substantiate a desirable determination.[43] This perception was recognized by Justice Marshall in 1973:

> It seems to me inescapably clear that this Court has consistently adjusted the care with which it will review state discrimination in light of the constitutional significance of the interests affected and the invidiousness of the particular classification. . . . The majority suggests, however, that a variable standard of review would give this Court the appearance of a 'super-legislature'. . . . I cannot agree. Such an approach seems to me a part of the guarantees of our Constitution and of the historic experience with oppression of and discrimination against discrete, powerless minorities which underlie that document. In truth, the Court itself will be open to the criticism raised by the majority so long as it continues on its present course of selecting in private which cases will be afforded special consideration without acknowledging the true basis of its action.[44]

In his review of constitutional law, Gunther indicated that one of the problems associated with the three tiered concept of scrutiny is that many perceive it as artificial, mechanical and perhaps even a bit dishonest.[45] Despite these perceptions, it is unlikely that this structure will be abandoned in the immediate future. Fortunately, substantive changes within the field of public health law have encouraged the use of definitive criteria in the selection of review standards and the examination of public health necessity.

Efforts to clarify the procedural components of the judicial review process within the field of public health have introduced a number of important standards that have direct bearing on the legal issues associated with AIDS.[46]. The imposition of a public health measure upon an individual requires substantial scientific evidence that the person actually has an infectious condition, that circumstances exist whereby the infection can be communicated, and that the measure would have an impact of eliminating or reducing the risk of contagion.[47] Although these requirements have helped to ameliorate some of the negative perceptions regarding the process of judicial inquiry, many conceptual problems still exist within

---

43. Gostin, *Traditional Public Health Strategies* in AIDS AND THE LAW, A GUIDE FOR THE PUBLIC 47 (H. L. Dalton and S. Burris eds. 1987).
44. San Antonio Indep. School Dist. v. Rodriquez, 411 U.S. 1 (1973) at 110.
45. G. GUNTHER, CONSTITUTIONAL LAW (11th ed. 1985) at 589.
46. Sicklick, *A Medical Review of AIDS (Law, Social Policy, and Contagious Diseases: A Symposium on AIDS)*, 14 HOFSTRA L. REV. 5 (1985).
47. Gostin, *Traditional Health Strategies* in AIDS AND THE LAW, A GUIDE FOR THE PUBLIC 52 (H. L. Dalton and S. Burris eds. 1987).

the law that make it difficult to insulate victims of communicable disease from the pervasive fear and ignorance that still remain within society.

The Formation of AIDS Policy: The Need for a Development Model

From the time that AIDS became a public health problem in 1981, numerous policies including screening, testing, reporting, contact tracing, isolation, and quarantine have been invoked to curtail the progress of the epidemic. The impact of many of these policies has allowed researchers to calibrate the progress of the epidemic, while others have limited efforts to bring the epidemic under control. Society has not encountered any epidemics of major infectious diseases since the polio outbreak of the 1950's. This good fortune means there is a lack of recent social and political experience in coping with such problems. In fact, it would be necessary to go back 70 years to the influenza pandemic of 1918 to find a pathogen as deadly as the AIDS virus. Social inexperience in dealing with complex social health problems has resulted in a health policy model deficiency that now hampers the nation's ability to cope in an effective manner with the AIDS crisis.

Despite an abundance of scientific and medical information concerning AIDS, inexperience in dealing with health problems of this magnitude and complexity has made many fearful and cautious, not unlike public responses to smallpox and polio. Conflicting information from the scientific and medical communities about the AIDS causative agent, reports about unconventional ways of contracting AIDS, as from a dentist, as well as a general confusion on the part of the public, have contributed to a defensible policy vacuum. Emotional responses to the AIDS epidemic have created an environment of uncertainty which is often denied by the larger society and tolerated by the scientists and medical persons. Catastrophic events at Three Mile Island, Kennedy Space Center, and Chernobyl, for example, have dramatically altered the public's perception regarding the authority and credibility of experts. As discussed in Chapter 3, many individuals believe that AIDS is more dangerous than the scientific community would have the general public believe.

Part of the problem in dealing with the dilemma created by AIDS is that society is not adept at comparing risks, especially where human lives are involved. The political culture within this country has been reticent historically to accept the explicit costs of certain policies even when there is a good chance of success. For example, as in the early 1900's with venereal disease, education has been presented as one of the few positive activities that might reduce the progress of the AIDS epidemic. Yet, some individuals view explicit sexual education as encouraging homosexual and licentious activity.[48] The prevalence of this view has impacted a variety of individuals from television executives to elected public officials. People seem unwilling to assume the risk of possibly offending the sensibilities of those who believe that educating the public about AIDS is an inappropriate or unethical response to the current crisis.

Policies that have little or no potential for reducing the spread of AIDS could have considerable legal, social and cultural appeal. Until more is done to separate realistic concern from irrational fear, the high mortality that is associated with AIDS could promote the implementation of inappropriate public health measures. Despite the preponderance of historical data rejecting such measures, the public is likely to sanction their implementation in light of the crisis of confidence that exists within the general population regarding the authority of scientific experts. As presented in Chapter 2, a review of the case law associated with the use of the police power in this country during the last century reveals that a vast majority of the cases within the field of public health have been decided under one or more legislative acts rather than under constitutional law. Although federal legislation has been particularly important to victims of debilitating diseases, such as AIDS, it has failed to provide ample policy guidance on how to cope with the tens of thousands of HIV-positive individuals among us whose rights may be jeopardized by reflexive actions grounded on fear, ignorance, and prejudice.

The need for a public school policy on AIDS is dependent on the actual or probable incidence of AIDS within any single school district. Although cases of AIDS have been reported in all fifty states, the District of Columbia, and three United States territories, most are among residents of large metropolitan areas or coastal cities. This finding implies that the majority of public school districts throughout the United States are relatively free of AIDS at the present time. One could assert that the demand for a viable public school AIDS policy is considerably less in those areas where the incidence of AIDS is low. A survey in 1988, however, involving a sample of 100 school superintendents from all over the country indicates that 97 percent of the respondents agreed that every school district should have a policy that focuses on students and adults with AIDS, even though 68 percent of respondents said that "they had no experience with (persons having) AIDS in their school district."[49]

---

48. Brandt, *AIDS in Historical Perspective: Four Lessons from the History of Sexually Transmitted Diseases*, 78 AM. J. PUB. HEALTH 367 (1988).
49. Keough and Seaton, *Superintendents' Views on AIDS: A National Survey*, 2 PHI DELTA KAPPEN 358 (1988).

Public school officials require an appropriate model or paradigm to pattern their efforts in addressing the plethora of issues associated with AIDS. The criteria and information that follow in Chapter 5 represent a synthesis of current scientific, legal, and policy information concerning AIDS as it applies to the educational environment. Collectively, this synthesis forms the basis for an effective policy model that can be used by educational administrators to resolve issues associated with AIDS within public schools.

CHAPTER V
An AIDS Policy Paradigm for Public Schools

Introduction

Acquired immunodeficiency syndrome (AIDS) represents one of the most complex and perplexing problems to materialize within the last 100 years. Since its identification in 1981, this disease has maintained a relentless and devastating attack on the American society. The epidemiological evidence presented earlier in Chapter Two is sobering. Unless steps are taken to check its future course, AIDS will undoubtedly consume a sizeable portion of this nation's human and economic resources. Efforts to control this disease have been complicated by the presence of complex moral, legal, and social problems that operate synergistically when combined. The resolution of these problems has generated considerable controversy within the fields of public health and law. Part of the debate centers upon the issue of regulations as they impact on individual autonomy. The formulation of an equitable balance between public and private rights is an arduous task that is complicated by public fear and ignorance regarding the societal impact of epidemic disease. These circumstances pose a significant challenge for policymakers who must contend with the conundrum of AIDS under the political imperative of protecting the health of society while maintaining the constitutional rights of those person afflicted with AIDS.

This chapter represents a synthesis of the preceding four chapters. The information contained in this chapter will help district policymakers answer the following questions: What scientific, legal, and social factors are important in the construction of an AIDS policy paradigm? How can districts facilitate the process of AIDS policy formation? How can districts evaluate their current AIDS policies? This chapter is divided into two major areas. The first part of the chapter focuses directly on the development of an AIDS policy paradigm. Many of the discussions will explain why specific scientific, legal, and social precedents are included in the model, and how they impact the overall effectiveness of educational policy as it pertains to students and adults with AIDS or HIV infection. The second part of the chapter provides information on how the AIDS policies of public school districts highly impacted by AIDS compare with the paradigm that is presented. The primary focus of this section is to establish the efficacy of the model by discussing its ability to facilitate an effective educational AIDS policy response as well as to examine existing school district AIDS policy.

Constructing a District AIDS Policy Paradigm

An analysis of the scientific, legal, and policy information concerning AIDS discloses the existence of various criteria that should be used in the construction of a school district AIDS policy. These criteria can be classified into three separate categories based on their impact within the educational environment (See Table 1). The first category of policy criteria is designated as "general"; it contains AIDS policy criteria which impact the entire educational community. The second category of policy criteria is designated as "student" and contains only those policy criteria which affect any individual who is entitled to attend a public school in grades kindergarten through high school (K-12), as well as any pre-kindergarten child who is entitled attendance at school. The third category of policy criteria is entitled "adult". This final category contains only those AIDS policy criteria which affect any teacher, administrator, food service worker, or other school staff member.

The effort to formulate an effective school district policy for AIDS necessitates that a variety of issues or inquiries be addressed within the process of policy development. These issues or inquiries may be considered as decision points within the process of policy formulation. Within the present policy model, these issues or inquiries are presented within the context of a school district AIDS policy decision matrix that is formulated with respect to the school district AIDS policy criteria presented in Table 1. The rationale behind this approach is two-fold. First, the process of formulating a school district policy for AIDS is difficult at best. It is important, therefore, to describe the decision-making process that is involved in the formulation of a legal and socially responsive school district model. Second, it is important that school districts be able to explain their policy formation processes and rationales in light of scientific and legal considerations to those concerned.

Articulation of the Model: General Characteristics

To expedite both understanding and use of the paradigm, various decision points and policy conclusions concerning AIDS and public education are depicted as different shapes within the decision matrix. Decision points are represented by ovals and are connected to either another decision point or to a policy outcome. Policy outcomes that are unsubstantiated by current scientific and legal reasoning are depicted as rectangles within the matrix (See Figure 2). Also much of the discussion that follows concerning either student or adult policy criteria is presented in more detail than is shown in the policy decision matrix. The decision to eliminate infor-

Table 1.   School District AIDS Policy Criteria

Policy Characteristics: General

AIDS Policy Developed by the School District
Separate District Policy Developed for AIDS
Universal Precautions versus HIV Testing
Differentiated AIDS Policy for Students and Adults
Case-by-Case Evaluation and Monitoring
Readmission Procedures for Students and Adults
Strict Confidentiality of Medical Information
Mandatory Reporting of Suspected HIV Carriers
Medical Evaluation of Suspected HIV Carriers
Notification of Teacher or Site Administrator

Policy Characteristics: Student

Provisions to Remove Student for Public Safety
Provisions to Remove Student for Personal Safety
Vaccine Exemptions for Students with AIDS or HIV Infection
Provisions for Alternative Education when Excluded
Specific Provisions for Special Education Students
Provisions to Evaluate Sports Participation
Provisions to Evaluate Participation in Vocational Classes

Policy Characteristics: Adults

Provisions to Remove Adults for Public Safety
Provisions to Remove Adults for Personal Safety
Provisions for Employee Accommodation
Specific Procedures for Food Service Workers

Figure 2. School District AIDS Policy Decision Matrix

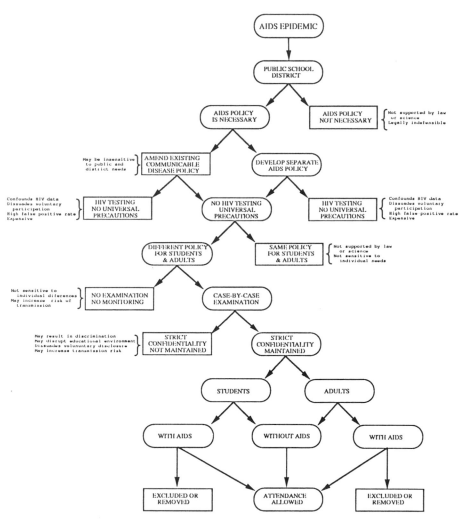

MAJOR POLICY OUTCOMES

mation from the figure depicting the decision matrix was made on the basis of clarity and space. Nonetheless, various policy issues and decision points were retained to illustrate major policy outcomes. The discussion also follows the school district AIDS policy criteria listed in Table 1.

District AIDS Policy is Necessary

The scientific evidence concerning the spread of AIDS cannot be overlooked. Having no policy for AIDS is no longer an option for school districts. Unfortunately, many public school officials admit that they have no experience in dealing with AIDS.[1] This experience deficit will undoubtedly frustrate efforts of many school districts that lack necessary resources to develop an effective local policy on AIDS. As a result, many districts will have to rely on some other institutional body to provide them with an effective AIDS policy that answers the specific needs of their district. For example, the Department of Education in New Jersey formulated a policy on AIDS that is being used in the Newark School District, one of the areas highly impacted by AIDS. Many school districts within the New York City area have also relied on an outside source, the Board of Cooperative Educational Services (BOCES), to create an appropriate policy response to AIDS.

The advantages gained by allowing another organization with greater resources to develop district policy are slightly offset by a number of problems that could encumber the policy once it has been implemented. First, policies that are developed outside the district may not be sensitive to the issues present within the local district. Depending on circumstances, policy insensitivity could result in the disparate treatment of specific groups or individuals within the district, thereby placing them and the district at greater risk. Second, administrative control over a policy typically resides at the point of policy formation. Unless the organization that developed the policy relinquishes administrative control over the policy, the local district may be unable to, or be reluctant to, make changes within the policy to respond quickly and efficiently to issues that surface within the district. Third, administrative control over a policy decreases as the distance between the point of policy formation and the point of policy implementation increases. This attenuation often occurs when the organization that developed the policy does not transfer appropriate administrative control over the policy to the local district.[2] Policies that exhibit this problem are often insen-

---

1. *Id.*
2. A Downs, Inside Bureaucracy (1967).

sitive to changes that occur within the local district. In comparison, policies that are developed locally reflect a greater understanding of changes within the district. Ownership of the policy is stronger and feedback on policy decisions is faster.

Separate District Policy Developed for AIDS

Since it is clear that the AIDS epidemic poses a significant health threat to society and to the educational environment, public school officials must respond to the existence of this disease by creating an appropriate AIDS policy within the district. The next decision to be addressed within the matrix is whether the district will amend an existing communicable disease policy to develop a separate policy covering persons with AIDS or persons who have been found to be HIV positive.

In a survey of school superintendents, 58 percent of respondents indicated that "school districts should not treat AIDS differently from other communicable diseases."[3] There are a number of educators who believe that AIDS is not a communicable disease in the technical sense because it is not casually communicated.[4] Like many members of the scientific community, these educators believe that the "theoretical" risks of transmission within the school setting do not warrant the attention that AIDS has been receiving within the print and electronic media. Policies that call attention to AIDS by treating it as a separate category, when that has yet to be established, only serve to exacerbate an already critical situation by fueling the firestorm of fear that has been ignited by the current pandemic. Based on this reasoning, one could assert that AIDS should not be considered as a separate policy issue; however, a more prudent course of action would be to rely on the judgment of professionals who have accumulated some experience in dealing with AIDS.

Numerous reports and publications by the Centers for Disease control, the National Education Association, and the American Academy of Pediatrics have advocated the development and implementation of policies that focus directly on the issue of AIDS within schools. In 1986, the National Education Association issued the following statement concerning AIDS policy development:

> Every school district, college, and university should establish
> guidelines for dealing with problems presented by students and
> employees who have or could transmit Acquired Immunodefi-

---

3. Keough and Seaton *supra* note 49, at 359.
4. Reed, *AIDS in Schools: A Special Report*, 67 PHI DELTA KAPPAN 494 (1986).

ciency Syndrome (AIDS) to other students or school employees. The organized employee organization should be involved in the development of these guidelines and any dispute as to their meaning or application should be subject to the appropriate grievance/arbitration procedure. The guidelines should be reviewed periodically and revised as necessary to reflect new medical information regarding AIDS.[5]

The scientific and legal reasons for the development of a separate AIDS policy have been well established.[6] The efforts made by Dade County (Florida) Public School System and Houston (Texas) Unified School District demonstrate that many of the recommendations concerning AIDS can be established within an already existing communicable disease policy framework.

There are, however, problems associated with the integrated policy approach which can help to explain why this approach has failed to achieve universal acceptance within school districts and the medical community. First, an integrated policy approach often obscures the actions and recommendations of policy officials regarding specific issues within the community. This obscurity makes it difficult for people to observe what has been done to resolve any one particular problem. Second, as discussed in Chapters 2 and 3, there is a great deal of controversy regarding the issue of AIDS within public schools. Many parents are noticeably concerned about the safety of their children with the school setting. When public concern is coupled with fear and ignorance, it often creates a potentially explosive situation in the community. This situation can only be defused when employees, parents, and students throughout the school district believe that specific steps have been undertaken by the school district to address their various concerns.

School officials must realize that educational policy can assume a variety of functions simultaneously within the district. In addition to its administrative function, an effective AIDS policy will also promote confidence within the school district and the community it serves. Confidence is an important element in the fight against AIDS. Unfortunately, many communities are in the midst of a crisis in confidence because of the AIDS epidemic. Experience has demonstrated that confidence will not emerge naturally from a policy that is not easily discernible from its surroundings. A school district is best served by a separate AIDS policy.

---

5. National Education Association, *Recommended Guidelines for Dealing with AIDS in the Schools*, 56 J. SCH. HEALTH 129 (1986).
6. McCormick, *Sound Policies And Expert Advice Are Your Best Protection Against AIDS*, AM. SCH. BD. J. 36 (May, 1986).

Universal Precautions versus HIV Testing

The issue of AIDS antibody testing will confront every school district sometime during the process of policy formation. The legal and social implications associated with mandatory serological testing of students and adults for the human immunodeficiency virus (HIV) in the public school setting have generated controversy among various segments of the population. Advocates of mandatory antibody testing assert that accurate information is necessary to curtail the spread of AIDS. Proponents also posit that the implementation of routine antibody testing will eliminate much of the stigma associated with AIDS, thereby allowing a greater number of infected individuals to seek medical treatment. In contrast, opponents believe that mandatory testing for AIDS would seriously impact current efforts to thwart the disease because it would deter the very people who need help most from coming forward for medical assistance and would undoubtedly place many individuals at risk of discrimination.

Ninety three percent of superintendents responding to the Keough and Seaton survey oppose mandatory serological testing for the AIDS virus of professional employees, support staff, students, or volunteers. Within the same survey, more than 78 percent of the respondents oppose contracts that either make serological testing for HIV a condition for employment or call for the dismissal of nontenured employees who test positive for HIV.[7] The conclusions presented by this survey concur with the finding of investigators at George Washington University who reported in 1987 that no state required either mandatory or routine HIV antibody screening for the general public.[8]

At the present time, no legal or scientific justification exists for mandatory HIV testing of students or adults within the educational environment. Based on this fact, it would be unwise for public school officials to construct a district AIDS policy around antibody testing. This does not, however, mean that public school officials should become complacent regarding AIDS. Public school officials should follow guidelines set forth by CDC regarding the establishment of "universal precautions" for preventing the transmission of bloodbourne infectious diseases, including the human immunodeficiency virus (HIV) and the hepatitis B virus (HBV) throughout the school district.[9] Once established, these precautions should be enforced routinely, as should other standard precaution for infection

---

7. Keough and Seaton *supra* note 49, at 359.
8. INTERGOVERNMENTAL HEALTH POLICY PROJECT, A SUMMARY OF AIDS LAW FROM THE 1986 LEGISLATIVE SESSIONS 4 (1987).
9. Centers for Disease Control, *Education and Foster Care of Children Infected With Human T-lymphotropic Virus Type III/Lymphadenopathy Associated Virus*, 34 MORBIDITY AND MORTALITY WEEKLY REPORT, 517 (1985).

control, regardless of whether employees or students are known to be infected with either HIV or hepatitis B virus. Public health officials also recommend that all students and adults receive information and training regarding the epidemiology, modes of transmission, and prevention of HIV infection.

Differentiated AIDS Policy for Students and Adults

The conclusions reached thus far indicate that as a result of the decision to adopt universal precautions rather than institute mandatory serological HIV testing, public school officials are confronted by the issue of whether a district AIDS policy should differentiate between students and adults with AIDS. The scientific information associated with AIDS indicates that the educational environment poses unique problems for epidemiologists. Researchers admit that their experience with the AIDS infection in school, day care, or foster care settings is limited. Based on their experience with other communicable diseases, however, a theoretical potential for transmission **does** exist within the educational environment. The magnitude of this transmission potential depends on a number of factors, including age, maturity level, neurological status, and physical condition which are clinically recognizable. The impact of these factors is not consistent over time or between students and adults. This makes it extremely difficult to consider adults and students similarly.

Based on these findings, members of the scientific and educational communities have recommended a policy approach that differentiates between students and adults.[10] The differentiated policy approach is sensitive to the differences observed between different school populations. Consideration is given to how these differences impact the theoretical risk of AIDS transmission within the public school setting.

Case-by-Case Evaluation and Monitoring

The differentiated policy approach also establishes a policy vehicle whereby students and adults can be evaluated individually on a case-by-case basis to determine the benefits, risk, and most appropriate educational placement or job classification. This particular approach can also provide a mechanism by which public schools officials can monitor the health and emotional status of infected students or employees.

---

10. *Id*. at 518; *see also*, National Educ. Ass'n, *supra* note 54, at 129.

The incidence of AIDS infection in children has been well established.[11] Transmission of the AIDS virus in children is limited to perinatal and parenteral transmission events. If casual transmission of the virus does exist, it should be more evident among younger children rather than adults and would likely involve exposure of one's open skin lesions or mucous membranes to blood and possibly other body fluids of an infected individual. Present scientific and medical findings, however, do not support such transmission. Given these findings, there is no prevailing medical or scientific evidence to support the automatic exclusion of HIV-infected students from public school. However, Centers for Disease Control (CDC) officials indicate that studies of transmission risks through contact between younger children and neurologically handicapped children who lack control of their bodily functions are limited. They recommend, therefore, that decisions regarding the type of educational placement and care of AIDS infected children should be deliberated on an individual basis ''using the team approach including the child's physician, public health personnel, the child's parent or guardian, and personnel associated with the proposed care or educational setting.'' In each case, ''the risks and benefits to both the infected child and to others in the setting should be weighed.''[12]

A policy position not based on case-by-case examination and monitoring is unsupportable for a number of reasons. First, public health officials have indicated that the educational environment provides an efficient conduit for disease transmission. Given this potential, it would be unwise for public school officials to ignore the presence of either older students or younger children with AIDS or HIV infection. Second, epidemiologists concede that their experience with AIDS among children is limited. As a result, public health officials have issued special recommendations concerning the placement of specific categories of children within the school. These recommendations can only be implemented on a case-by-case basis. Third, blanket policy approaches may actually augment the personal and public health risks associated with the AIDS epidemic. Such all inclusive policies are insensitive to the normal variations which occur within the schools or within the victims themselves.

Readmission Procedures for Students and Adults

Routine screening or testing of adults and students for the serological presence of HIV as a condition for employment within the school district,

---

11. Ammann and Shannon, *Recognition of Acquired Immunodeficiency Syndrome (AIDS) in Children*, 7 PED. REV. 101 (1985); Rogers, *AIDS in Children: A Review of the Clinical Epidemiologic and Public Health Aspects*, 4 PED. INFECT. DIS. 230 (1985).
12. Centers for Disease Control, *supra* note 58, at 518.

or for admission or readmission to school is not recommended by public health officials and may be legally construed as an unwarranted personal intrusion. School districts may, however, as part of a medical review process, institute procedures for the evaluation of the physical and psychological status of any adult or student with AIDS prior to their return to work or school. The precedent for this criterion was established in 1979 when the Supreme Court determined that an employer is not obligated to continue the employment of an individual whose psychological or physical status makes reasonable job performance impossible.[13] Although this decision could have a devastating effect on the victims of AIDS, its impact in this application is mitigated by the fact that victims of handicapping illnesses are protected under federal law, as discussed in Chapter 3. Therefore, the intention of the medical review process should not be to exclude the adult or student with AIDS; rather the intention should be to provide the best employment or educational opportunity possible considering the exigencies of the situation and the severity of the affliction.[14] In many instances, this task can be best handled by the district health officer who can act as liaison with the appropriate medical personnel and coordinate the services provided by the school district.

Strict Confidentiality of Medical Information

The goal of the individualized approach to placing HIV-positive students or adults within the public school setting is to provide a quality educational experience for students, and as normal a work setting as possible for adults. Because of the volatile nature of the AIDS issue and concern displayed by members of the school and community, possible reactions by those involved could create a climate that is counterproductive to this goal. As public health officials have observed, "the diagnoses of AIDS or AIDS-related illnesses evoke much fear from others in contact with the student and may evoke suspicion of lifestyles that may not be acceptable to some individuals."[15] Such reactions would be possible only if the presence of an infected student or adult is widely known. Therefore, the identity of a student or adult with AIDS should not be publicly revealed. The number of personnel aware of the student's or co-worker's condition or suspected condition should be kept to the minimum necessary to assure

---

13. Southeastern Community College v. Davis, 442 U.S. 397, 99 S. Ct. 2361, 60 L.Ed.2d 345 (1979).
14. *See also*, Board of Educ. v. Cooperman, 209 N.J. Supp. 174, 507 A.2d 253 (1986).
15. Centers for Disease Control, *supra* note 58, at 519.

proper care of the individuals and to detect situations in which the potential for transmission may increase. Persons involved in the care of an HIV-infected student "should be sensitive to the need for confidentiality and the right to privacy in these cases."[16]

As the incidence of AIDS continues to expand into the public schools, an increasing number of educational personnel will have to deal with the tension between the duty to disclose pertinent medical information concerning AIDS to protect other members of society and the responsibility to safeguard the confidentiality of personal medical information. This is a critical issue for all public school employees who teach, interact or care for AIDS victims.[17] In the final analysis, the impact of the AIDS epidemic upon the educational community will depend on the balance that is struck between these two opposing interests.[18]

The jurisprudence regarding the issue of confidentiality is not absolute.[19] Although courts have repeatedly held that the duty of nondisclosure is outweighed in certain circumstances by the need for public safety, there has been an effort to identify the conditions under which this information is to be disclosed and by whom.[20] In 1987, Lewis reported that 17 states had enacted specific legislation to protect the confidentiality of AIDS-related medical and research information.[21]

Many parents are reluctant to reveal the HIV status of their children to public health and school officials because of the intense publicity and harassment that has often resulted from such disclosures. Some parents are painfully aware of the isolation that can result when the HIV status of a child becomes known to others within the school. In the absence of any statutory requirement, school officials should create a substantive and procedural policy framework that ensures the confidentiality of medical and personal information.

Information pertaining to the medical and HIV status of any student should be released only if the parent or person legally authorized to con-

16. *Id.*
17. Fleming and Maximov, *The Patient or His Victim: The Therapist's Dilemma*, 62 CAL. L. REV. 1025 (1974); George, Korin, Quattrone, and Mandel, *The Therapist's Duty to Protect Third Parties: A Guide for the Perplexed*, 14 RUTGERS L. J. 637 (1983); Roth and Meisel, *Dangerousness, Confidentiality, and the Duty to Warn*, 134 AM. J. PSYCH. 508 (1977).
18. Anderson, *AIDS-Related Litigation: The Competing Interests Surrounding Discovery of Blood Donors' Identities*, 19 IND. L. REV. 561 (1986).
19. Nanula, *Protecting Confidentiality in the Effort to Control AIDS*, 24 HARV. J. ON LEGIS. 315 (1987).
20. Belitsky and Solomon, *Doctors and Patients Responsibilities in a Confidential Relationship* 201 in AIDS AND THE LAW, A GUIDE FOR THE PUBLIC (H. L. Dalton and S. Burris eds. 1987).
21. Lewis, *Acquired Immunodeficiency Syndrome: State Legislative Activity*, 258 J. AM. MED. A. 2411 (1987).

sent for the student voluntarily releases or discloses the information or authorizes release or disclosure of medical information. Similarly, information pertaining to the medical or HIV status of adults within the school should be released only if the individual voluntarily releases the medical information or authorizes the release or disclosure of the information. In either case, authorization must be in writing and must indicate the persons or entities or classification of persons or entities to whom the results may be released or disclosed. As required by law, medical information may be released to local or state public health officials for the purpose of surveillance. The coordination and release of such information should be the responsibility of the district health officer. The district health department should also act as a clearinghouse and distribution point for information received pertaining to the AIDS epidemic or its causative agents.

The importance of maintaining strict confidentiality in all matters related to AIDS cannot be overemphasized. Failure to adopt a policy of maintaining strict confidentiality when dealing with personal health information may actually augment the potential for AIDS transmission within the schools. When faced with the realization that disclosure of their HIV status may result in acts of prejudice and discrimination against them, victims of AIDS may hide their illness from public school officials. This subversive behavior effectively insulates them from the remainder of the school district AIDS policy. The positive effects of the policy, which would otherwise occur if strict confidentiality was maintained, are negated by the fact that people are avoiding the very help they need. As a result, these infected individuals will remain undetected and unmonitored within the educational community, but the health risks to themselves and others remain.

Mandatory Reporting of Suspect HIV Carriers

The impact of undetected or unmonitored HIV-positive individuals within the educational environment is significant considering the magnitude of this disease and the hysteria it promotes within society. All school employees within the district should, therefore, be directed to immediately report any information indicating that a student or adult within the school system has, or is suspected of having, HIV infection. Although the impact of this policy directive could have negative repercussions if strict confidentiality is not maintained, the rationale behind its implementation is to preserve and protect the health of the person with AIDS as well as the public. The current scientific and medical evidence suggests that individuals who are afflicted with HIV may experience varying degrees of immune dysfunction. As a result, these persons are more susceptible to opportunistic infections and diseases which occur frequently within the educational environment. Based on the scientific evidence that indicates that HIV exhibits a variable incubation period, it is quite possible that a person could be infected with the virus and be unaware of their serological status. Thus, an established AIDS reporting procedure is necessary to protect the health of the individual and to provide an appropriate educational or employment placement when necessary.

Medical Evaluation of Suspected HIV Carriers

If an individual suspected of being an HIV carrier is reported to the school district health officer, the district health officer should discreetly attempt to verify the accuracy of the information by initiating the appropriate contacts. If the district health officer has reasonable cause to believe that the student or employee identified in the report received is infected with HIV, the district should require the individual to undergo an appropriate medical evaluation. Although this policy initiative appears controversial, there is legal precedence for its existence. Under the provisions of the tenth amendment to the U.S. Constitution, state legislatures may require certain medical requirements, such as vaccinations or health examinations, as a condition of school attendance or employment. An examination of this issue in Chapter 3 revealed that courts have generally viewed school attendance requirements as a valid exercise of state police power. No constitutional rights are abridged by such legislation as the right to attend school is necessarily subject to certain limitations and restrictions in the interest of the public health.[22] Victims of AIDS or HIV infection, however, may be legally protected from such action under the Rehabilitation Act of 1973 if it can be shown that the results obtained in a medical evaluation were used to screen out victims of handicapping illnesses. Many of the negative aspects of this dilemma can be avoided if the school district initiates substantive procedures to ensure that any information that is obtained or disseminated in this process remains confidential. The information should be restricted to only those individuals who have a legitimate need to know in order to verify the information received or to provide appropriate serves one the report has been confirmed.

Notification of Teacher or Site Administrator

When an individual with AIDS or HIV infection is know to be present within the educational environment either by personal disclosure or

---

22. Zucht v. King, 225 S.W. 267 (Tex. Civ. App. 1920); Pierce v. Board of Educ., 30 Misc. 2d 1039, 219 N.Y.S.2d 519 (App. Div. 1961).

by medical examination, the district health officer should notify those persons with whom the seropositive individual will interact closely on a daily basis. The law of confidentiality is critically important to the success of the initiative. Parents who fail to inform public school officials that their child is afflicted with AIDS because they fear harassment or discrimination may be placing their child and perhaps other children at risk of infection. Although public health officials assert that for the majority of children with AIDS, "the benefits of an unrestricted setting would outweigh the risks of their acquiring potentially harmful infections in the setting", they also recognize that children with AIDS are a "greater risk of suffering severe complications from such infections as chicken pox, cytomegalovirus, tuberculosis, herpes simplex, and measles."[23] Thus, it is critical that someone within the school, such as the principal, school nurse, or teacher of record, be informed that a student with AIDS is present within the school. Public health officials also point out that the parents of children with AIDS are more inclined to disclose such information when an environment of acceptance, confidence, and respect exists within the community.[24]

Articulation of the Model: Specific Characteristics

The process of AIDS policy formation becomes more complicated when the questions and issues begin to focus upon specific population groups within the educational setting. The school population can be subdivided into two principal population groups: students and adults. Each of these two groups exhibits a unique set of physical and psychological characteristics which differentiate them as either students or adults. Because these characteristics are rarely congruous, there is a need within the process of policy formulation to examine each one of these population groups as separate entities. The deliberation should attempt to determine those areas where either the rights of students to an education or the rights of adults to work will be affected by the compelling need to ensure the health and safety of all.

Much of the detail that exists within public school AIDS policy today was established in response to either personal or public health issues concerning students and adults with AIDS. Personal health issues are identified as those concerns a student or adult with AIDS would have to face as a participant within the educational setting. Personal health concerns can focus on a variety of issues including: alternate educational oppor-

23. Centers for Disease Control, *supra* note 58, at 518.
24. Centers for Disease Control, *supra* note 58, at 517.

tunities for students with special needs or during outbreaks of communicable diseases, vaccination exemptions for students, and special accommodations for adults with special needs or during outbreaks of communicable diseases. In contrast, public health issues are those concerns that focus on the preservation of public health. They can include: special procedures for food service workers, reporting procedures, provisions to evaluate parental requests for student participation in vocational education classes or in sports, provisions to remove infectious students or adults from the educational environment, and district re-entry procedures for students and adults.

Many of the school district AIDS policy criteria that pertain to either students or adults within the model will be presented here in more detail than is shown within the AIDS policy decision matrix (See Figure 2). The school district AIDS policy criteria associated with students are presented first and then succeeded by the school district AIDS policy criteria for adults.

AIDS Policy Criteria Associated with Students

Provisions to Remove Students for Public Safety

There is sufficient scientific and legal evidence to suggest that persons with contagious diseases may be removed from the school by appropriate members of the district in order to prevent further transmission of the disease.[25] The authority to remove students for public health reasons is not, however, absolute. By virtue of their illness, students with AIDS are protected under federal laws which prohibit discrimination against the handicapped. School districts should resort to this remedy only when the nature or severity of the disease is such that education in regular classes can not be achieved satisfactorily.

The rationale behind the individualized approach is to provide the student with AIDS or HIV infection with an educational experience that is as normal as possible. Public school officials should design and adopt appropriate procedures to routinely monitor all persons who are identified as having AIDS or HIV infection. Depending on the circumstances and the individual involved, this task can be best handled by the school nurse or district health officer who acts as liaison with the appropriate medical personnel and coordinates the services provided by the staff and district. In particular, students with AIDS should be monitored continuously in order to determine whether their behavior or medical condition has changed in such a way as to affect their ability to communicate HIV to others. Students

---

25. Centers for Disease Control, *supra* note 58, at 517; *see* Pierce v. Board of Educ., 30 Misc. 2d 1039, N.Y.S.2d 519 (App. Div. 1961); Community High School Dist. 155 v. Denz, 124 Ill. App. 3d 129, 463 N.E.2d 998 (1984).

that are removed from classroom attendance because of open lesions, ill-ness, or inimical behavior should be monitored as necessary to determine whether the condition precipitating the exclusion has abated.

Provisions to Remove Students for Personal Safety

Students with AIDS may exhibit varying degrees of immune suppres-sion which makes them more susceptible to opportunistic infections and diseases within the public school. As a result, students with AIDS may be excluded from classroom attendance or school for their own protection when cases of acute or short-term communicable diseases, such as measles or chicken pox, are occurring within the school population. At such times, the school site administrator or the school nurse should notify the appropriate district and public health officials, as well as the physician and parent of the immunodeficient student. Recommendations regarding the attendance or educational placement of HIV-positive students during outbreaks of in-fectious diseases should be made on an individual basis by the educational placement review board.

Vaccine Exemptions for Students with AIDS

Medical researchers have indicated that the immunological abnor-malities associated with symptomatic HIV infection raises concerns about the immunization of infected children. Because of their clinical status, the "replication of live, attenuated vaccine viruses may be enhanced in persons with immunodeficiency diseases and theoretically may produce severe adverse events following immunization...."[26] Based on the ex-igencies of their illness, children with symptomatic HIV infections should not be required to receive live-virus and live-bacterial vaccines. Public health officials also recommend that "for routine immunizations, these persons should receive inactivated polio vaccine and should be excused for medical reasons for regulations requiring measles, rubella, and/or mumps immunization."[27]

Provisions for Alternate Education when Excluded

There is sufficient legal precedent to suggest that whenever a student with AIDS is temporarily excluded from classroom attendance, either to protect the student or to reduce the risk of transmission, an alternative educa-

---

26. Centers for Disease Control, *Immunization of Children Infected With Human T-lymphotropic Virus Type III/Lymphadenopathy Associated Virus*, 35 MORBIDITY AND MORTALITY WEEKLY REPORTS 598 (1986).
27. *Id.* at 603.

tional program should be provided.[28] The school principal where the student normally attends classes should be responsible for coordinating and monitoring such special programming. If the student is expected to be removed from the classroom for an extended period of time (**e. g.**, longer than ten days), arrangements should be made for the student to receive homebound educational services.

Specific Procedures for Special Education Students
It is anticipated that some students with AIDS or HIV infection may already be receiving special education within the school district. Public health officials have voiced concern regarding the educational placement of neurologically handicapped children, particularly those children who lack control of their body secretions or display inimical behavior.[29] As required by law, the special needs of exceptional students are met through an individualized educational plan (IEP) that is designed using a team approach and implemented by the school district. The special educational needs of exceptional students with AIDS who are allowed to attend or remain in school should be determined by the teacher of record in accordance with federal and state laws and regulations. Provisions for exclusion because of medical reasons should be included as an eventuality on the students's IEP. Exceptional students with AIDS who are excluded or removed from classroom attendance for medical reasons should receive special education for the homebound or the appropriate educational placement. The placement and progress of these students should be continuously monitored by the school district.

Provisions to Evaluate Sports or Vocational Education Participation
The physical and psychological requirements for participation in either sports or vocational education classes are similar. Although there is little scientific or medical information available on AIDS concerning either of these activities, reasonable people can assume there is a greater health risk associated with certain sports and vocational education classes. Public school officials should, therefore, evaluate on an individual basis requests to participate in these activities for students with AIDS or HIV infection. Decisions should be made in cooperation with the student's parents and physician. In making this determination, school officials should consider the infected student's behavioral characteristics, neurological develop-

---

28. Board of Education of the Hendrick Hudson Cent. School Dist. v. Rowley, 458 U.S. 176 (1982).
29. Centers for Disease Control, *Education and Foster Care of Children Infected With Human T-lymphotropic Virus Type III/Lymphadenopathy Associated Virus*, 34 MORBIDITY AND MORTALITY WEEKLY REPORT 517 (1985) at 520.

ment and physical condition, and the expected type of interaction the student will have with other students in the sport or class. If approval is granted, arrangements should be made for the clean up of blood spills and body fluids as recommended by public health officials.

AIDS Policy Criteria Associated with Adults

Provisions to Remove Adults for Public Safety

The circumstances and conditions surrounding the placement or employment of adults with AIDS or HIV infection are less compelling than those observed for students within the school setting because of differences in age, maturity level, and neurological status that are observed between these two groups. Many of the epidemiological models that are used to assess the relative risk of transmission within specific environments, such as schools, depend on the existence and magnitude of these observable differences. Realizing these differences, public health officials assert that based on their experience with other communicable agents, such as the hepatitis B virus, the theoretical potential for transmission would be greatest among younger preschool children and neurologically handicapped children who lack control of their bodily secretions.[30] Given this information, the theoretical risk of transmission for adults should be considerably less than the risk for younger students within the same environment. Hence, there is no current scientific or medical evidence to support the automatic exclusion or termination of public school employees for reasons of AIDS or HIV infection.

As in the case of students, the determination of whether an employee with AIDS or HIV infection should be permitted to remain employed in a capacity that involves contact with students or other school employees should be made on an individual basis utilizing a team approach involving members of the public health community, the school employee and/or legal representative, the employee's physician, and appropriate school district personnel. In making the determination, the team should consider: (1) the risk to the employee including, but not limited to, physical condition, immune status, stamina, degree of handicap, and ability to perform job-related duties in the assigned situation; and, (2) the possible risk to other adults or employees that arise from behavior, open lesions, and infections.

Employees who are excluded from the educational setting for reasons of public safety should be monitored by the district health officer to determine whether the condition precipitating the exclusion has abated.

---

30. *Id*. at 519.

Employees returning to duty should be readmitted by the district health officer following any period of exclusion or hospitalization.

Provisions to Remove Adults for Personal Safety

The goal behind the individualized approach to the dilemma of employees with AIDS or HIV infection within the public school environment is to provide the necessary support and assistance to enable the employee to continue working for as long as possible. The attainment of this goal can only be accomplished within a climate where acceptance, respect, and privacy are nurtured and protected by public school officials. The school district should establish routine administrative procedures that can be applied: (1) when an immunodeficient employee may need to be absent from work for personal health reasons when cases of acute or short-term communicable diseases, such as measles or chicken pox, are occurring within the school population; (2) when there is a question of whether an individual is physically or emotionally capable of performing his or her duties as an employee of the public school system; (3) when there is a question of disruption of the efficient operation of the school necessitating an involuntary transfer; and, (4) when there is a request for a voluntary transfer by an employee with AIDS or HIV infection.

Employees who are absent or temporarily removed from duty because of open lesions, illness, or outbreaks of infectious diseases within the school population should be monitored by the district health officer to determine whether the condition precipitating the absence or removal has abated. Employees returning to duty should be readmitted by the district health officer following any disease-related absence. In the event that employment of an infected school employee is discontinued, the school system should allow the employee to use any available medical leave and to receive any available medical disability benefits.

Specific Procedures for Food Service Workers

Food service employees with AIDS or HIV infections should not be restricted from work unless they have evidence of other infection or illness for which any food service employee should also be excluded. Researchers working at the Centers for Disease Control report that "all epidemiological and laboratory evidence indicates that blood-borne and sexually transmitted infections are not transmitted during the preparation or serving of food or beverages, and no instances of HBV (hepatitis B virus) or HTLV-III/LAV transmission have been documented in this setting."[31]

---

31. Centers for Disease Control, *Recommendations for Assisting in the Prevention of Perinatal Transmission of Human T-lymphotropic Virus Type III/Lymphadenopathy Associated Virus and Acquired Immunodeficiency Syndrome*, 34 MORBIDITY AND MORTALITY WEEKLY REPORT 681 (1985) at 694.

School officials should design and adopt appropriate strategies to monitor conditions and procedures associated with the preparation and serving of food and beverages within the public school district. All food service employees should follow recommended standards and practices of good personal hygiene and food sanitation. All food service employees should exercise care to avoid injury to hands when preparing food. Should an injury occur, both aesthetic and sanitary considerations dictate that food contaminated with blood be discarded appropriately.

Provisions for Employee Accommodation

Various efforts to exclude adult victims of AIDS or HIV infection from the education setting are not supported by either the science or the law associated with the disease. Employers are required by law to make reasonable accommodation for a disabled employee unless it can be shown that such accommodation would impose an undue hardship on the employer.[32] The possible approaches that could be used by a school district in accommodating the victims of AIDS are as diverse as the people involved. Typically, a school district could accommodate victims of AIDS by providing alternative job sites, alternative work responsibilities, extended leave, or paid medical leave. However, school district employees should not be required to teach, interact, or provide other personal contact services with any HIV seropositive person unless the infected individual has been cleared by an appropriate placement review board.[33]

Employees who believe that they are at risk of infection because of their own immune status should be encouraged to discuss their work duties and responsibilities with their personal physician. In the event that a determination is made that there are assignments that the employee should not accept due to specific medical reasons, these facts should be communicated in writing to the district health officer for appropriate action. Employees who refuse to perform their assigned duties for reasons other than personal health should be examined on an individual basis in accordance with district administrative policy or local union contract.

At the present time, pregnant school employees are not known to be at greater risk of contracting HIV infection than are individuals who are not pregnant.[34] However, if an employee develops HIV infection during pregnancy, the infant is at risk of contracting HIV through perinatal transmission. Because of this risk, pregnant employees or students should

---

32. School Board of Nassau County v. Arline, 772 F.2d 759, 764 (11th Cir. 1985) *aff'd*, 107 S. Ct. 1123 (1987).

33. National Educ. Ass'n, *Recommended Guidelines for Dealing with AIDS in the Schools*, 56 J. SCH. HEALTH 129 (1986).

34. Centers for Disease Control, *supra* note 80, at 721 & 731.

be especially familiar with and strictly adhere to blood and body-fluid precautions to minimize the risk of HIV transmission. Employees should be encouraged to discuss any concerns they may have regarding their pregnancy or personal health with their physician. Pregnant students can be removed to an alternative educational site where the student could receive counseling and medical assistance in coping with the physical and psychological aspects of pregnancy.

Major AIDS Policy Outcomes

Every school district within the United States will have to decide whether a school policy on AIDS is warranted. To many competent observers, this decision has already been made for public school districts by the epidemic itself. Over 50 percent of the 15,681 school districts nationwide have some form of AIDS policy that allows students and adults with AIDS or HIV infection to enter or to remain within the school setting.[35] However, in spite of this, there are school districts that have adopted the contrary policy position whereby students and adults with contagious diseases, such as AIDS, are automatically excluded from public school attendance or employment.[36]

Although it may appear that a priori decisions regarding the exclusion of individuals with AIDS or HIV infection may be appealing and seem to be the safest approach to the AIDS epidemic, such an expedient policy is unwise for two reasons. First, there is a preponderance of legal, scientific and medical evidence that suggest that both students and adults with AIDS or HIV infection should be allowed to enter and to remain within the public school environment. Second, a policy excluding AIDS-linked students and adults from school will force infected adults and the parents of infected students to hide their illness from public school officials. This subversive behavior could have an impact upon the theoretical risk of transmission within the school and would undoubtedly prove to be counterproductive to the overall effort to curtail the future progress of the epidemic.

A Comparative Analysis of Selected District AIDS Policies

Notwithstanding the fact that AIDS is a national problem, school district response concerning this pandemic has been varied. Conceivably, the response of many school districts to the AIDS crisis has been predicated on a number of social and political factors, the most compelling of which has been the presence of either students or adults with AIDS within the

35. *AIDS and Children*, CITY AND STATE 6 (Jan. 18, 1988).
36. Reed, *AIDS in Schools: A Special Report*, 67 PHI DELTA KAPPAN 4949 (1986).

school district. Unfortunately, the task of policy development has been difficult for many educators because they possess neither the expertise nor the experience to effectively deal with the issues formed by the AIDS crisis. As a result, many administrators feel like coxswains whose boats are adrift in a fog bank. Unable to see, they wait for a beacon of light to guide their craft away from the rocky shoal to safe harbor.

Nonetheless, experience can play an important role in the development of public policy. As indicated earlier in this chapter, the process of AIDS policy development in this country has been hampered by our lack of experience in dealing with major epidemic health problems. However, certain states, cities, and school districts within this country have gained considerable experience in dealing with AIDS since it was identified in 1981. The experience of school districts in dealing with AIDS within highly impacted areas of the country is particularly germane to the task of school district policy development because it provides a valuable historical perspective on this disease as well as its impact upon the educational environment. Their experience in dealing with AIDS may also be used to test the efficacy of the paradigm currently under consideration.

The epidemiological data concerning the incidence and location of reported AIDS medical cases within the United States since June of 1981 indicate that the majority of the reported cases of AIDS have been clustered in five states: New York (24.7% of all AIDS cases), California (21.1%), Florida (7.6%), New Jersey (6.9%) and Texas (6.7%). Collectively, these five states account for more than 67 percent of the total number of cases of AIDS reported to public health officials nationally.[37] According to Centers for Disease Control (CDC) officials, the seven standard metropolitan statistical areas (SMSA) that have reported the greatest number of AIDS cases include: New York City (22.1% of all AIDS patients), San Francisco (8.4%), Los Angeles (7.6%), Houston (3.2%), Newark (3.0%), Washington, DC (3.0%), and Miami (2.5%). The following school districts have been identified within six of those cities: Manhattan Borough High School District (MBHSD), San Francisco Unified School District (SFUSD), Los Angeles Unified School District (LAUSD), Houston Unified School District (HUSD), Newark School District (NSD), and Dade County Public Schools (DCPS).

Using the school district AIDS policy paradigm developed in this chapter as a comparative framework, an analysis was conducted on each of six school district AIDS policies obtained for this analysis. As was done previously, the various criteria that should be utilized in formulating a district

---

37. Centers for Disease Control, *AIDS Weekly Surveillance Report - United States*, 37 MORBIDITY AND MORTALITY WEEKLY REPORT 1 (Aug. 15, 1988).

policy for AIDS have been classified into three distinct categories: general, student, and adult. To expedite the comparative process, the issues or characteristics observed within each school district AIDS policy are discussed in relation to the AIDS policy decision matrix which was constructed around the AIDS policy criteria identified earlier. The following discussion will begin at the top of the decision matrix and then move down toward the three major policy conclusions located at the bottom of the matrix. The major findings of this analysis are presented in Table 2.

Statistical projections involving the AIDS virus indicate that at some point in the progression of this disease, every school district will have to respond to the presence of either students or adults with AIDS within the educational environment. Faced with this eventuality, the question of whether or not a school district should develop an effective policy for AIDS seems absurd considering the magnitude of the present crisis. All six of the school districts chosen have responded to the AIDS epidemic by establishing some form of policy that considers the presence of persons with AIDS within the educational environment.

As observed earlier, the process of formulating an effective school district AIDS policy is made more difficult by the fact that many school districts have little experience in dealing with a major health crisis. Without this experience, many school districts may find themselves embroiled in a legal or political controversy over AIDS. Fortunately, school districts can rely on other sources or organizations to assist them in responding to the AIDS crisis. An examination of the six school district AIDS policies chosen for this analysis indicates that the Newark School District as well as the Manhattan Borough High School District have obtained their AIDS policies from sources outside their districts. In the case of these two school districts, relying on outside policy sources may be an efficient means to expedite the process of policy formation when dealing with more than one school district within the same city.

After the decision has been made that a school district AIDS policy is necessary, the next policy issue to consider is whether the AIDS policy should exist as a separate entity or be incorporated into another already existing communicable disease policy. Although some controversy exists concerning this issue, officials at the Centers for Disease Control and the National Education Association advocate policies that focus upon AIDS as a separate biological entity within the educational environment. A review of the six school district AIDS policies indicates that four of the public school districts have chosen to identify AIDS as a separate policy issue despite the fact that AIDS may exhibit certain epidemiological similarities to other communicable diseases. Two other school districts, Dade County Public Schools and the Houston Unified School District, have decided

Table 2. Selected School District AIDS Policy Characteristics

POLICY CHARACTERISTICS	SELECTED SCHOOL DISTRICTS					
GENERAL	MBHSD	SFUSD	LAUSD	HUSD	NSD	DCPS
AIDS Policy Developed by the School District	No	Yes	Yes	Yes	No	No
Separate District Policy Developed for AIDS	Yes	Yes	Yes	No	Yes	No
Universal Precautions Instead of HIV Testing	Yes	Yes	Yes	Yes	Yes	Yes
Differentiated AIDS Policy for Students & Adults	Yes	Yes	Yes	Yes	Yes	Yes
Case-by-Case Evaluation & Monitoring	Yes	Yes	Yes	Yes	Yes	Yes
Strict Confidentiality of Medical Information	Yes	Yes	Yes	Yes	Yes	Yes
Readmission Procedures for Students & Adults			Yes			
Mandatory Reporting of Suspected AIDS Carriers				Yes		
Medical Evaluation of Suspected AIDS Carriers	Yes					
Notification of Teacher or Site Administrator	Yes	Yes		Yes		
STUDENTS						
Provisions to Remove Students for Public Safety	Yes	Yes	Yes	Yes	Yes	Yes
Provisions to Remove Students for Personal Safety		Yes	Yes	Yes		
Vaccine Exemptions for Students with AIDS or HIV		Yes	Yes			
Provisions for Alternative Education when Excluded	Yes	Yes	Yes	Yes	Yes	Yes
Specific Procedures for Special Ed. Students			Yes	Yes		
Provisions to Evaluate Sports Participation			Yes			
Provisions to Evaluate Participation in Voc. Classes						
ADULTS						
Provisions to Remove Adults for Public Safety	Yes		Yes		Yes	
Provisions to Remove Adults for Personal Safety		Yes	Yes	Yes		
Specific Procedures for Food Service Workers						
Provisions for Employee Accommodation				Yes		

Legend: Manhattan Borough High School District (MBHSD)
            San Francisco Unified School District (SFUSD)
            Los Angeles Unified School District (LAUSD)
            Houston Unified School District (HUSD)
            Newark School District (NSD)
            Dade County Public Schools (DCPS)

Note: Blanks indicate no explicit policy statement on the issue.

instead to incorporate many of the suggestions presented by the Centers for Disease Control concerning AIDS or HIV within their existing communicable disease policies.

The legal and social ramifications associated with mandatory HIV testing are particularly germane to the process of school district AIDS policy development. Presently, there is no rational basis available to support mandatory testing of either students or adults within the educational environment. None of the six public school districts surveyed maintain a policy that requires either students or adults to undergo HIV testing. In the place of mandatory HIV testing, these six public school districts have adopted the recommendations set forth by the Centers for Disease Control concerning the establishment of universal precautions for the prevention of communicable disease transmission.

The question of whether or not students and adults should be treated separately in terms of AIDS policy development is especially important considering the differences that exist between these two population groups. As discussed earlier, public health officials are reluctant to state that the transmission potential for certain categories of students is nonexistent. Therefore, a more prudent course of action for school districts would be to formulate a school district policy that differentiates between students and adults on the basis of clinically recognizable features, such as age, maturity level, neurological status, and physical condition. An examination of the school district AIDS policies solicited indicates that all six school districts have adopted a differentiated policy approach whereby students and adults can be evaluated on a case-by-case basis to determine the benefits, risks, and most appropriate educational placement or job classification.

During the process of AIDS policy development, districts will have to respond to the issues that are associated with the confidentiality of student and employee health records. Circumstances over the last fifty years demonstrate that widespread disclosure of confidential medical information concerning AIDS or its causative agent would place people at risk of discrimination and seriously undermine the atmosphere of trust that exists within many school district. The accumulated epidemiological data on AIDS indicate that for most nonmedical learning or working environments, the risk of acquiring AIDS through casual contact with an infected person is extremely remote. Based on these data, public health officials recommend that information concerning the HIV status of any person within the district should be restricted only to those persons who have a compelling need to know in order to provide case and to detect situations where the potential for HIV transmission may increase.[38]

---

38. Centers for Disease Control, *supra* note 78, at 520.

Although most educators agree with the recommendations presented by public health officials regarding the issue of confidentiality, some disagreement exists within the educational community regarding the disclosure of medical information to either teachers or school principals. A significant portion of this controversy has been fired by the fears of educators who have allowed their emotions to overpower their intellect. Emotions aside, officials at the Centers for Disease Control as well as the National Education Association agree there are sound personal and public health reasons to support disclosure of confidential medical information to specific members of a school or worksite when an individual with AIDS is known to be present. An examination of the six school district AIDS policies selected indicates that although all six of the school district policies concerning AIDS adhere to strict confidentiality regarding the disclosure of personal medical information. Only three (Manhattan Borough High School District, San Francisco Unified School District, Houston Unified School District) of the six school districts routinely inform either the primary teacher or the site administrator when a student or adult with AIDS is known to be present within the educational environment.

The effort to formulate an effective school district AIDS policy becomes more demanding when the concerns begin to focus upon either students or adults. Each of these two groups exhibits a unique set of physical and psychological characteristics which differentiates them as either students or adults. In fact, much of the detail that is observed within public school AIDS policy today has materialized in response to these characteristics. An analysis of the six school district AIDS policies obtained reveals that many of the concerns regarding these two disparate population groups are associated with either personal or public health issues. As explained previously, personal health issues are those concerns that a student or adult with AIDS would have to face as a participant or employee within the school district. In contrast, public health issues focus on those concerns that are associated with the preservation of public health.

Within the area of public health, an evaluation of the school district policies selected reveals that although all six school districts have an explicit policy regarding the removal of infected students who pose a significant public health risk, only three (Manhattan Borough High School District, Los Angeles Unified School District, Newark School District) maintain a similar policy for infected adults. On the personal health side of this issue, three school districts (San Francisco Unified School District, Los Angles Unified School District, Houston Unified School District) have a provision that allows students or adults to move to an alternate educational or employment site during outbreaks of infectious disease, such as measles or chicken pox. Within this group, only the Los Angles Unified School District has an established policy for the evaluation of students or adults when they re-enter the district following a health-related absence.

Within the area of student health, members of the public health community have raised some concerns regarding the negative effects of vaccines on students with AIDS. Despite numerous recommendations by the Centers for Disease Control, the medical rationale behind vaccination exemptions for students with AIDS has failed to achieve wide acceptance within the educational community. This conclusion is supported by the fact that only two (San Francisco Unified School District, Los Angeles Unified School District) of the six policies examined here allow vaccination exemptions for students with AIDS.

There are a issues associated with AIDS that can precipitate a myriad of legal and social problems for inexperienced school officials. For example, the Houston Unified School District has incorporated a procedure for the reporting of suspected HIV carriers within its school district AIDS policy. Similarly, the Manhattan Borough High School District has adopted a policy provision that requires suspected HIV carriers within the district to undergo medical evaluation. Although there is ample support for these two initiatives, their implementation may actually attenuate the effectiveness of a school district AIDS policy if strict confidentiality of personal health information is not mandated and maintained throughout each process.

The last issue examined within the context of the policy paradigm is the controversy that has materialized with respect to public school cafeterias. Understandably, many parents have been concerned about the possibility that either students or food service workers with AIDS could communicate the AIDS virus to other individuals within the cafeteria setting. Public health officials have responded to those concerns by issuing recommendations for preventing transmission of the AIDS virus within the work place and specifically within the food service industry.[39] To date, none of the school districts reviewed has an explicit AIDS policy concerning either food service workers or food preparation.

A district policy model must have real empirical referents if the model is to be congruent with reality. A school district policy model for AIDS should be able to identify those processes and features that actually exist in the real world. With that purpose clearly defined, analysis of the six school district AIDS policies reveals the existence or absence of various policy features which have been examined in relation to the three categories of criteria contained within the AIDS policy paradigm (See Table 2 at page 95).

---

39. Centers for Disease Control, *supra* note 78, at 520.

Figure 3. School District AIDS Policy -- Decision Path 1

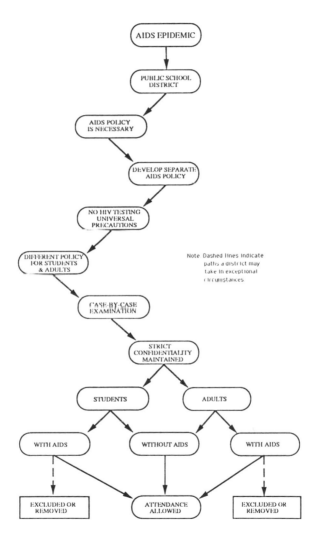

<u>Figure</u> 4. School District AIDS Policy -- Decision Path 2

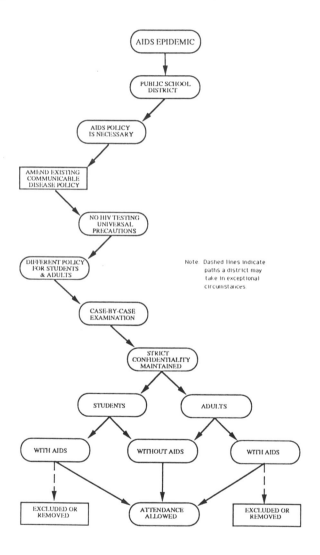

<u>Figure</u> 5. School District AIDS Policy -- Decision Pathways

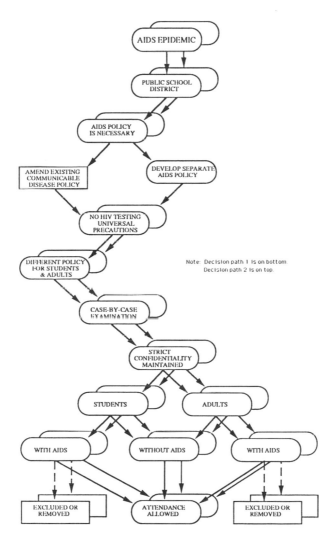

The process of policy formation involves the resolution of a variety of critical issues that are associated with one major dilemma. When the process of policy development is viewed from beginning to end, each critical issue locates a decision point along a chain of events that is referred to as a decision pathway. An analysis of the school district AIDS policies here discussed reveals the existence of two decision pathways that are formed by the six school districts in developing their respective AIDS policies (See Figures 3 and 4). Further analysis indicates that four (Los Angeles Unified School District, Manhattan Borough High School District, Newark School District, San Francisco Unified School District) of the six school districts followed **Decision Path 1** and two (Dade County Public Schools, Houston Unified School District) followed **Decision Path 2** in formulating their respective AIDS policies.

In many respects, numerous similarities exist among the six school districts. Generally, they all evolved from the same data base. However, the important issue here is whether these six school district AIDS policies are totally accommodated within the district AIDS policy paradigm created in this monograph. Analyses of the policies reveal that all of the critical issues that exist within the school district policies were covered by the model. A comparison between the two decision pathways and the district policy decision matrix demonstrates that the school district AIDS policy model developed here is congruent with school district practices (See Figure 5). Therefore, it is clear that the paradigm developed for this monograph not only facilitates the process of AIDS policy development, but also is useful in the evaluation of school district AIDS policies as they exist within areas impacted with AIDS and having already formulated, by whatever means, an AIDS policy.

Conclusions

The exigency for a public school district policy on AIDS is dependent on the actual or probable incidence of AIDS within any specific school district. Although AIDS has been reported throughout the United States, most of the cases have been clustered within large metropolitan areas or coastal cities. On that basis, one could argue that the demand for a viable school district AIDS policy is significantly less in those areas where the number of cases remains low. It is reasonable, however, to assume that as the threat of AIDS continues its inexorable expansion into the American society, an increasing number of public school officials throughout the United States will be forced to respond to the AIDS crisis.

Approximately 50 percent of the public school districts nationwide have some form of AIDS policy that allows persons with AIDS or HIV infection to remain within the educational environment. There are a number of school districts, however, that have adopted the counter position of not allowing persons with AIDS or HIV infection to remain within the schools. Although this latter position may be politically appealing and seem to be the safest approach in dealing with the AIDS epidemic, such an expedient policy is unwise for two reasons. First, there is a preponderance of scientific and legal evidence to indicate that persons with AIDS or HIV infection should be allowed to enter or remain within the public school system. Second, a policy of excluding infected persons will force the victims into a position where they must hide their affliction from school officials in order to enter or to remain within the schools.

The process of AIDS policy formation within the schools hinges upon the ability of educational administrators to resolve effectively the conflicts that exist among various interest groups. Many public school officials, unfortunately, have found they have neither the experience nor the expertise to cope with the present health crisis. Like many of their urban counterparts, these public school officials will have to rely on sources other than their own district for policy guidance. Although there may be some problems concerning administrative control and policy sensitivity with this approach, relying on outside sources may be an efficient means to expedite policy formation when dealing with large metropolitan areas, such as New York, where more than one school district exists within the same city.

In an effort to expedite the process of policy formation, some school districts have incorporated the Centers for Disease Control recommendations concerning the prevention of AIDS within an existent communicable disease policy. Although this would appear to be an effective method to accommodate the AIDS crisis within many systems, numbers of individuals within the scientific and educational communities contend that this approach does not promote clarity, comprehension, or confidence within the school district. When public concern about AIDS is coupled with fear and ignorance, it often creates an explosive climate within the community. This situation can only be defused when people understand that specific steps have been taken by the school district to protect the health and safety of both students and adults.

Both legal and social controversy are associated with the mandatory testing of students or adults for AIDS. Although the proponents of AIDS testing assert that accurate epidemiological information is needed to control the epidemic, there are no current legal or scientific bases to support this argument. It seems unwise for educational administrators to create a school district AIDS policy around AIDS testing. Public school officials, however, must recognize the likelihood that some persons with AIDS or HIV infection may not be known to district personnel. Therefore, public school officials should establish universal precautions for preventing the transmission of blood-borne infectious diseases throughout the district.

Although the current epidemiological information about AIDS indicates that none of the identified cases of HIV infection is known to have been transmitted in the school, day-care, or foster-care setting, public health officials admit to limited experience. Theoretically, if casual transmission of the AIDS virus does exist in these environments, it should be more evident among younger children rather than adults, and would most likely involve exposure of open skin lesions or mucous membranes to blood or other body fluids of an infected person. Given this potential, decisions concerning the type of educational placement and care of AIDS virus positive children should be deliberated on a case-by-case basis using a team approach.

The goal behind the individualized approach to the problem of placing the student with AIDS or AIDS virus infection within the school is to provide an educational experience as normal as possible. Because of the volatile nature of the AIDS crisis and the concern displayed by members of the school and community, possible reactions by those involved could create a climate that would be counterproductive to the aim of providing a normal education. Such reactions would be possible only if the presence of an infected person is widely known. Therefore, the identity of a student with AIDS should not be publicly revealed and the number of district personnel informed should be kept to the minimum necessary to assure proper care of the student and to detect situations in which the potential for transmission may increase.

Much of the detail that exists within district AIDS policy today was created in response to issues within the areas of personal and public health. Legally, the rights of students and adults with AIDS must be protected. There are no scientific or legal bases for exclusion of infected persons. The conclusions drawn by the medical and scientific communities, as well as the legal community, support an individualized approach to the problem of AIDS. Accordingly, school officials should implement procedures to provide: (1) alternative educational opportunities for students with special needs, (2) vaccination exemptions for infected students and adults, and (3) alternative employment opportunities for infected adults whenever events warrant their implementation in order to protect the personal health of any student or adult with AIDS. Public school officials should institute specific procedures to: (1) monitor all food preparation areas, (2) evaluate requests for sport or vocational education class participation, (3) remove individuals who, because of their behavior or personal health, pose a greater risk of transmitting the AIDS virus within the school setting, and (4) monitor entry and reentry of HIV positive students and adults within the school in an effort to preserve the public health.

Public school officials should arm themselves with competent legal, scientific, and policy advice that is available when confronting the potential medical, social, and emotional problems associated with AIDS. Although there is an abundance of scientific and legal information available on the subject of AIDS, information alone will not solve the dilemma of whether persons with AIDS or AIDS infection should be allowed to attend classes or work within the school system. Given the magnitude of this problem, it is conceivable that many public school officials throughout the country are searching for an appropriate policy model to pattern their efforts in responding to the diverse issues associated with AIDS. Accordingly, a suitable school district policy paradigm, which represents a synthesis of the current legal, medical, and scientific thought on the nature of AIDS, has been established. In the final analysis, however, educational administrators must rely on their knowledge, experience, and compassion in dealing with either students or adults who have AIDS. Realizing that much of the pain and suffering associated with this devastating disease is created by the perceptions of others within society, public school officials must consciously and consistently strive to resolve the tension between individual and public rights.

TABLE OF CASES

BIBLIOGRAPHY

Articles and Books Cited

Aaron, H. J. (1978). Politics and the professors: The great society in perspective. Washington, D.C: The Brooking Institute.

A band-aid for AIDS. (1988, August 6). Miami Herald. p.22A.

Ahluwalia, I. B. (1988). The epidemiology of AIDS. In K. D. Blanchet, AIDS: A health care management response (pp. 31-53). Maryland: Aspen Publications.

AIDS and children. (1988, January 18). City and State. p. 6.

AIDS test examined. (1988, July 2). The Economist. pp. 70-71.

AIDS victim to return to school. (1986, February 20). USA Today. p. A-2.

American Academy of Pediatrics, Committee on School Health, Committee on Infectious Diseases. (1986). School attendance of children with human T-lymphotropic virus III/lymphadenopathy associated virus infection. Pediatrics, 77, 430-432.

Ammann, A. J. (1985). The acquired immunodeficiency syndrome in infants and children. Annals of Internal Medicine, 103, 734.

Ammann, A. J. & Shannon, K. (1985). Recognition of acquired immunodeficiency syndrome (AIDS) in children. Pediatric in Review, 7, 101-107.

Anderson, D. C. (1986). AIDS-related litigation: The competing interests surrounding discovery of blood donors' identities. Indiana Law Review, 19, 561-587.

Bayer, R., Levine, C., & Murray, T. H. (1986). Guidelines for confidentiality in research on AIDS. In M. D. Witt (Ed.), AIDS and patient management: Legal, ethical, & social issues (pp.) 72-86. Owing Mills, MD: National Health Publishing.

Barnes, D. M. (1986). Grim projections for AIDS epidemic Science, 232, 1589.

Barnes, D. M. (1987). Sex and needles, not insects and pigs spread AIDS in Florida town. Science, 234, 415-417.

Barre-Sinoussi, F., Cherman, J. C., Rey, F., Nugeyre, M. T. Chamaret, S., Gruest, J., Dauguet, C., Axler-Shin, C., Brun-Vezinet, F., Rouzioux, C., Rosenbaum. W., & Montagnier, L. (1983). Isolation of T-lymphotropic retrovirus from a patient at risk for acquired immnodeficiency syndrome. Science, 220, 868-871.

Baum, R. M. (1984, January). AIDS researchers track an elusive foe. Chemical & Engineering News. pp. 15-18.

Bayley, A. C., Cheingsong-Popov, R., Dalgleish, A. G., Downing, R. G., Tedder, R. S., & Weiss, R. A. (1985). HTLV-III serology distinguishes atypical and endemic Kaposi's sarcoma in Africa. Lancet, 1, 359-361.

Bazell, R. (1983, August). The history of an epidemic: An epidemic of myths and misperceptions. New Republic. pp. 14-18.

Belitsky, R. & Solomon, R. A. (1987). Doctors and patients responsibilities in a confidential relationship. In H. L. Dalton & S. Burris (Eds.), AIDS and the law, a guide for the public (pp. 201-209). New Haven: Yale University Press.

Benn, S., Rutledge, R., Folks, T., Gold, J., Baker, L., McCormick, J., Feorino, P., Piot, P., Quinn, T., & Martin, M. (1985). Genomic heterogeneity of AIDS retroviral isolates from North America and Zaire. Science, 230, 949-951.

Biggar, R. J., Melbye, M., Kestens, L., Sarngadharan, M. G., DeFeyter, M., Blattner, W., Gallo, R. C., & Gigase, P. L. (1984). Kaposi's sarcoma in Zaire is not associated with HTLV-III infection. New England Journal of Medicine, 311, 1051.

Blanchet, K. D. (1988). AIDS: A health care management response. Rockville, MA: Aspen.

Blattner, W.A., Biggar, R. J., Weiss, S. H., Melbye, M., & Goedert, J. J. (1985). Epidemiology of human T-lymphotropic virus type III and the risk of acquired immunodeficiency syndrome. Annals of Internal Medicine, 103, 655-670.

Bolognese, D. P. & Fischinger, P. J. (1985). Prospects for treatment of the human retrovirus-associated diseases. Cancer Research, 45, 4700s-4705s.

Booth, W. (1987). AIDS and insects: If you can get AIDS from sharing needles, why not from mosquitoes? Science, 237, 355-356.

Boyer, W. W. (1964). Bureaucracy on trial: Policymaking by government agencies. Indianapolis: Bobbs-Merrill.

Brandt, A. M. (1987). A historical perspective. In H. L. Dalton & S. Burris (Eds.), AIDS and the law, a guide for the public (pp. 37-43). New Haven: Yale University Press.

Brandt, A. M. (1988). AIDS in historical perspective: Four lessons from the history of sexually transmitted diseases. American Jounal of Public Health, 78, 367-371.

Breo, D. L. (1983). AIDS poses complex research puzzle, say New York investigators. American Medical News, 26, 1- 5.

Broder, S., Bunn, P. A., Jaffe, E. S., & Rogers, M. F. (1984). T-cell lymphoproliferative syndrome associated with human T-cell leukemia/lymphoma virus. Annals of Internal Medicine, 100, 543-545.

Broder, S., & Gallo, R. C. (1984). A pathogenic retrovirus (HTLV-III) linked to AIDS. New England Journal of Medicine, 311, 1292.

Brun-Vezinet, F. B., Rouzioux, C., Montagnier, L., Chamaret, S., Gruest, J., Barre Sinoussi, F., Geroldi, D., Chermann, J. C., McCormick, J., Piot, P., Taelman, H., Mirlangu, K. B., Kalambayi, K., Mazebo, P., Cridts, C., Desmyter, J., Feinsod, F. M., & Quinn, T. C. (1984). Prevalence of antibodies to lymphadenopathy associated with retrovirus in African patients with AIDS. Science, 226, 453-456.

Bygbjerg, I. C. (1983). AIDS in a Danish surgeon (Zaire, 1976). Lancet, 1, 925.

Byrom, N. A., Davidson, G., Draper, C. C., & Zuckerman, A. J. (1973). Role of mosquitoes in transmission of Hepatitis B antigen. Journal of Infectious Diseases, 128, 259- 260.

Campbell, A. M. (1976, June). How viruses insert their DNA into the DNA of the host cell. Scientific American. pp. 100-108.

Centers for Disease Control. (1981). Kaposi's sarcoma and pneumocystis pneumonia among homosexual men - New York City and California. Morbidity and Mortality Weekly Report, 30, 305-308.

Centers for Disease Control. (1981). Follow-up on Kaposi's sarcoma and pneumocystis pneumonia. Morbidity and Mortality Weekly Report, 30, 409-410.

Centers for Disease Control. (1981). Pneumocystis pneumonia: Los Angeles. Morbidity and Mortality Weekly Report, 30, 250-252.

Centers for Disease Control. (1982). Persistent, generalized lymphadenopathy among homosexual males. Morbidity and Mortality Weekly Report, 31, 249-252.

Centers for Disease Control. (1982). Update on Kaposi's sarcoma and opportunistic infections in previously healthy persons - United States. Morbidity and Mortality Weekly Report, 31, 294-301.

Centers for Disease Control. (1982). Update on acquired immune deficiency syndrome (AIDS) United States. Morbidity and Mortality Weekly Report, 31, 507-514.

Centers for Disease Control. (1982). Unexplained immunodeficiency and opportunistic infections in infants - New York, New Jersey, California. Morbidity and Mortality Weekly Report, 31, 665-667.

Centers for Disease Control. (1984). Antibodies to retrovirus etiologically associated with acquired immunodeficiency syndrome (AIDS) in populations with increased incidences of the syndrome. Morbidity and Mortality Weekly Report, 33, 377-379.

Centers for Disease Control. (1985). Education and foster care of children infected with human T-lymphotropic virus type III/lymphadenopathy associated virus. Morbidity and Mortality Weekly Report, 34, 517-521.

Centers for Disease Control. (1985). Recommendations for assisting in the prevention of perinatal transmission of human T-lymphotropic virus type III/lymphadenopathy-Aassociated virus and acquired immunodeficiency syndrome. Morbidity and Mortality Weekly Report, 34, 681-686, 721-722.

Centers for Disease Control. (1986). Apparent transmission of human T-lymphotrophic virus type III/lymphadenopathy-Aassociated virus from a child to a mother providing health care. Morbidity and Mortality Weekly Report, 35, 76-79.

Centers for Disease Control. (1986). Classification system for human T-lymphotropic virus type III/lymphadena-pathy associated virus infections. Morbidity and Mortality Weekly Report, 35, 334-339.

Centers for Disease Control. (1986). Immunization of children infected with human T-lymphotropic virus, type III/lymphadenopathy associated virus. Morbidity and Mortality Weekly Report, 35, 595-598, 603-606.

Centers for Disease Control. (1986). Acquired immunodeficiency syndrome (AIDS) in Western Palm Beach County, Florida. Morbidity and Mortality Weekly Report, 35, 609-612.

Centers for Disease Control. (1986). Acquired immunodeficiency syndrome (AIDS) among blacks and Hispanics - United States. Morbidity and Mortality Weekly Report, 35, 655-658, 663-666.

Centers for Disease Control. (1986). Acquired immunodeficiency syndrome: United States. Mortality and Morbidity Weekly Report, 35, 756-766.

Centers for Disease Control. (1987). Human immunodeficiency virus infection in transfusion recipients and their family members. Morbidity and Mortality Weekly Report, 36, 137-140.

Centers for Disease Control. (1987). Antibody to human immunodeficiency virus in female prostitutes. Morbidity and Mortality Weekly Report, 36, 157-161.

Centers for Disease Control. (1987). Update: Human immunodeficiency virus infections in health care workers exposed to blood of infected patients. Morbidity and Mortality Weekly Report, 36, 285-289.

Centers for Disease Control. (1987). Revision of the CDC surveillance case definition for acquired immunodeficiency syndrome. Morbidity and Mortality Weekly Report, 36, No. 1S, 1-15.

Centers for Disease Control. (1988). The extent of AIDS and indicators of adolescent risk. Morbidity and Mortality Weekly Report, 37, No. S-2, 10-13.

Centers for Disease Control. (1988). Quarterly report to the domestic policy council on the prevalence and rate of spread of HIV and AIDS in the United States. Morbidity and Mortality Weekly Report, 37, 223-226.

Centers for Disease Control. (1991). AIDS weekly surveillance report - United States. Morbidity and Mortality Weekly Report, 40, January 15, 1-5.

Chamberland, M. E., Castro, K. G., Haverkos, H. W., Miller, B. I., Thomas, P. A., Reiss, R., Walker, J., Spira, T. J., Jaffe, H. W., & Curran, J. W. (1984). Acquired immunodeficiency syndrome in the United States: An analysis of cases outside high-incidence groups. Annals of Internal Medicine, 101, 617-623.

Chase, C. (1986, May 30). AIDS is causing far more illness than the official figures convey. Wall Street Journal. p. 23.

Chelf, C. P. (1981). Public policymaking in America. Santa Monica, CA: Goodyear.

Chiado, F., Ricchie, E., Costigiola, P., Michealacci, L., Reade, M. C., & Gotti, D. (1986, June). Vertical transmission of LAV/HTLV-III. Paper presented at the Second International Conference on AIDS, Paris, France. Church, G. (1985, September). Not an easy disease to come by. Time. p. 27.

Clark, M., & Coppola, V. (1985, April 29). AIDS: A growing pandemic? Newsweek. p. 71.

Clavel, F., Guetard, D., Brun-Vezinet, F., Chamaret, S., Rey, M. A., Santos-Ferreira, M. O., Laurent, A. G., Dauguet, C., Katlama, C., Rouzioux, C., Klatzmann, D., Champalimaud, J. L., & Montagnier, L. (1986). Isolation of a new human retrovirus from west African patients with AIDS. Science, 233, 343-346.

Clumeck, N., Mascart-Lemone, F., deMaubeuge, J., Brenez, D., & Marcelis, L. (1983). Acquired immunodeficiency syndrome in black Africans. Lancet, 1, 642.

Clumeck, N., Vande Perre, P., Carael, M., Pouvroy, D. V., & Nzaramba, D. (1985). Heterosexual promiscuity among African patients with AIDS. New England Journal of Medicine, 313, 182.

Coffin, J., Haase, A., Levy, J. A., Montagnier, L., Oroszian, S., Teich, N., Temin, H., Toyoshima, K., Varmus, H., Vogt, P., & Weiss, R. (1986). Human immunodeficiency viruses. (letter). Science, 232, 697.

Comment. (1984). AIDS: A legal epidemic. Akron Law Review, 17, 717.

Cooper, D., Johnson, & Gold, J. (1986). Postnatal transmission of AIDS-associated retrovirus from mother to infant. Lancet, 1, 896.

Cooper, D. A., Maclean, P. Finlayson, R., Michelmore, H. M., Gold, J., Donovan, B. Barnes, T. G., Brooke, P., & Penny, R. (1985). Acute AIDS retrovirus infection: Definition of a clinical illness associated with seroconversion. Lancet, 1, 537-540.

Council of Chief State School Officers. (1988, June). AIDS education needs. AIDS Education Bulletin Board. p. 1.

Cowan, M. J., Hellmann, D., Chudwin, D., Wara, D. W., Chang, R. S., & Ammann, A. J. (1984). Maternal transmission of acquired immune deficiency syndrome. Pediatrics, 73, 382-A386.

Curran, J. W., Gostin, L., & Clarke, M. (1986). Acquired immunodeficiency syndrome: Legal, regulatory, and policy analysis. (U. S. Dept. Health and Human Services, No. 282-86-0032. Washington, D.C.

Curran, J. W., Lawrence, D. N., Jaffe, H., Kaplan, J. E., Zyla, L. D., Chamberland, M., Weinstein, R., Lui, K. J., Schonberger, L. B. Spira, T. J., Alexander, W. J., Swinger, G., Ammann, A., Solomon, S., Auerbach, D., Mildvan, D., Stoneburmer, R., Jason, J-M., Haverkos, H. W., & Evatt, B. L. (1984). Acquired immunodeficiency syndrome (AIDS) associated with transfusions. New England Journal of Medicine, 310, 69-75.

Curran, J. W., Morgan, W. M., Hardy, A. M., Jaffe, H. W., Darrow, W. W., & Dowdle, W. R. (1985). The epidemiology of AIDS: Current status and future prospect. Science, 229, 1352.

Dahl, K., Martin, K., & Miller, G.(1987). Differences among human immunodeficiency virus strains in their capacities to induce cytolysis or persistent infection of a lymphoblastoid cell line immortalized by Epstein-Barr virus. Journal of Virology, 61, 1602-1608.

Daniel, M. D., Letvin, N. L., King, Jr., N. W., Kannagi, M., Sehgal, P. K., Hunt, R. D., Kanki, P. J., Essex, M., & Desrosiers, R. C. (1985). Isolation of T-cell tropic HTLV-III-like retrovirus from macaques. Science, 228, 1201-1204.

Dauer, C., Korns, R., & Schuman, L. (1968). Infectious Diseases. Cambridge, MA: Harvard University Press.

Department of Health, Education, and Welfare. (1978). Food service sanitation manual. (DHEW Publication No. FDA 78-A2081. Washington, D.C.: U.S. Government Printing Office.

Dlutowski, J. M. (1986). Employment Discrimination: AIDS victims. Harvard Journal of Law & Public Policy, 9, 739-751.

Dole, R. (1973). Congressional Records, 119, 24589.

Dover, T. E. (1979). An evaluation of immunization regulations in light of religious objections and the developing right of privacy. University of Dayton Law Review, 4, 401-424.

Dowdle, W. (1986). The search for an AIDS vaccine. Public Health Reports, 101, 232-233.

Downs, A. (1967). Inside Bureaucracy. Boston: Little Brown Book Company.

Dror, V. (1969). Public policy reexamined. San Francisco: Chandler.

Drotman, C. P. (1985). Insect-borne transmission of AIDS? Journal of the American Medical Association, 254, 1085.

Dunn, W. N. (1981). Public policy analysis: An introduction. Engelwood Cliffs, NJ: Prentice Hall.

Dye, T. R. (1984). Understanding public policy. Engelwood Cliffs, NJ: Prentice-Hall.

Eales, L. J., Parkin, J. M., Forster, S. M., Nye, K. E., Weber, J. N., Harris, J. R. W., & Pinching, A. J. (1987). Association of different allelic forms of group specific component with susceptibility to and clinical manifestations of human immuno-deficiency virus infection. Lancet, 1, 999-1002.

Easton, D. (1965). A framework for political analysis. Engelwood Cliffs, NJ: Pentice-Hall.

Eckert, R. D. (1985, October). AIDS and the blood supply. Consumers' Research Magazine. pp. 20-25.

Education for All Handicapped Children Act. 20 U S C §§ 1400-1461 (West 1982 & Supp. III, 1985), 34 C.F.R. § 300.5 (b) (7), (1986).

Edwards, D. D., & Beil, L. (1988). Pessimistic outlook in AIDS reports. Science News, 133, 372.

Essex, M., & Kanki, P. J. (1988, October). The origins of the AIDS virus. Scientific American. pp. 64-71.

Essex, M. & Trainin, Z. (1981). Immune response to tumer cells in domestic animals. Journal of American Veterinary Medicine Association, 181, 1125.

Evatt, B. L., Ramsley, R. B., Lawrence, D. N., Zyla, L. D., & Curran, J. W. (1984). The acquired immunodeficiency syndrome in patients with hemophilia. Annals of Internal Medicine, 100, 499-504.

Fauci, A. S., & Fischinger, P. J. (1988). The development of an AIDS vaccine: Progress and promise. Public Health Reports, 103, 230-236.

Fischinger, P. J., Robey, W. G., Koprowski, H., Gallo, R. C., & Bolognese, D. P. (1985). Current status and strategies for vaccines against diseases induced by human T-cell lymphotropic retroviruses (HTLV-I, -II, -III). Cancer Research, 45, 4694s-4699s.

Feorino, P. M., Jaffe, H. W., Palmer, E., Peterman, T. A., Francis, D. P., Kalyan-araman, V. S., Weinstein, R. A., Stoneburner, R. L., Alexander, W. J., Raevsky, C., Gretchell, J. P., Warfield, D., Haverkos, H. W., Kilbourne, B. W., Nicholson, J. K. A., & Curran, J. W. (1985). Transfusion-associated acquired immunodeficiency syndrome: Evidence for persistent infection in blood donors. New England Journal of Medicine, 312, 1293-1296.

Fischl, M. A., Dickinson, G. M., Scott, G. M., Klimas, N., Fletcher, M. A., & Parks, W. (1987). Evaluation of heterosexual partners, children, and household contacts of adults with AIDS. Journal of the American Medical Association, 257, 640-644.

Fisher, A. G., Collati, E., Ratner, L., Gallo, R. C., & Wong-Staal. (1985). A molecular clone of HTLV-III with biological activity. Nature, 316, 262.

Fleming & Maximov. (1974). The patient or his victim: The therapist's dilemma. California Law Review, 62, 1025- 1033.

Fox, D. M. (1987). Physicians versus lawyers: A conflict of cultures In H. L. Dalton & S. Burris, AIDS and the Law, A Guide for the Public (pp 210-217). New Haven: Yale University Press

French scientists report discovery of AIDS virus in African insects. (1986, August 27). New York Times, p. A-10

Friedland, G. H., & Klein, R. S. (1987). Transmission of the human immunodeficiency virus. The New England Journal of Medicine, 317, 1125-1135.

Friedland, G. H., Saltzman, B. R., Rogers M. F., Kahl, P. A., Lesser, M. L., Mayers, M. M., & Klein, R. S. (1986). Lack of transmission of HTLV-III/LAV infection in household contacts of patients with AIDS or AIDS-related complex with oral candidiasis. New England Journal of Medicine, 314, 344-349.

Fujikawa, L. S., Salahuddin, S. Z., Palestine, A. G., Masur, H., Nussenblatt, R. B., & Gallo, R. C. (1985). Isolation of human T-lymphotropic virus type III from the tears of a patient with acquired immune deficiency syndrome. Lancet, 2, 529-530.

Gallo, R. C. (1987, January). The AIDS virus. Scientific American. pp. 47-56.

Gallo, R. C. (1986, December). The first human retrovirus. Scientific American. pp. 88-98.

Gallo, R. C., & Montagnier, L. (1988, October). AIDS in 1988. Scientific American. pp. 40-51.

Gallo, R. C., Salahuddin, S. Z., Popovic, M., Shearer, G. M., Kaplan, M., Haynes, B. F., Palker, T. J., Redfield, R., Oleske, J., Safai, B., White, G., Foster, P., & Markham, P. D. (1984). Frequent detection and isolation of cytopathic retroviruses (HTLV-III) from patients with AIDS and a risk for AIDS. Science, 224, 500-503.

Gallo, R. C., & Wong-Staal, F. (1985). A human T-lymphotropic retrovirus (HTLV-III) as the cause of acquired immune deficiency syndrome. Annals of Internal Medicine, 103, 679-689.

George, Korin, Quattrone, & Mandel. (1983). The therapist's duty to protect third parties: A guide for the perplexed. Rutgers Law Journal, 14, 637-645.

Gerberding, J. L., Bryant-LeBlanc, C. E., Nelson, K., Moss, A. R., Osmond, D., Chambers, H. F., Carlson, J. R., Drew, W. L., Levy, J. A., & Sande, M. A. (1987). Risk of transmitting the human immunodeficiency virus, cytomegalo-virus & heptatis B virus to health care workers exposed to AIDS & AIDS-related conditions. Journal of Infectious Diseases, 156, 1-8.

Gershwin, D. (1969). Towards a theory of public budgetary decision making. Administrative Science Quarterly, 14, 33-46.

Giron, J. (1985, September 19). Doctor wants teachers warned of AIDS pupils. Los Angeles Times, p. I-18.

Glaser, V. (1988, January). AIDS crisis spurs hunt for new tests. High Technology Business. pp. 34-39.

Gleason, J. A. (1986). Quarantine: An unreasonable solution to the AIDS dilemma. Cincinnati Law Review, 55, 217- 235.

Goedert, J., & Blattner, W. (1985). The epidemiology of acquired immune deficiency syndrome. In Devita, V., Hellman, S., & Rosenberg, S. (Eds.), AIDS: Etiology, diagnosis, treatment, and prevention (pp. 1-30). New York: J. B. Lippencott Company.

Gold, M. (1987, April). AIDS what we now know. McCalls. pp. 143-150.

Gonda, M. A., Wong-Staal, F., & Gallo, R. C. (1985). Sequence homotogy and morphologic similarity of HTLV-III and visnavirus, a pathogenic lentivirus. Science, 227, 173.

Gostin, L. (1986). Aquired immune deficiency syndrome: A review of science, health policy, and law. In In M. D. Witt (Ed.), AIDS and patient management: Legal, ethical, & social issues (pp. 3-20). Owing Mills, MD: National Health Publishing.

Gostin, L. (1987). Traditional public health strategies. In H. L. Dalton & S. Burris, AIDS and the Law, A Guide for the Public (pp.) 47-65. New Haven: Yale University Press.

Grint, P. & McEvoy, M. (1985). Two associated cases of the acquired immunodeficiency syndrome (AIDS). Communicable Disease Report, 42, 4.

Groopman, J. E., Cho, E., Oleske, J. M., Wong-Staal, F., & Gallo, R. C. (1985). HTLV-III infection in brains of children and adults with AIDS encephalopathy. Science, 6, 177.

Guinan, M. E. & Hardy, A. (1987). Epidemiology of AIDS in women of the United States. Journal of American Medical Association, 257, 2039-2042.

Guinan, M. E., Thomas, P. A., Pinsky, P. F., Goodrich, J. T., Selik, R. M., Jaffe, H. W., Haverkos, H. W., Noble, G., & Curran, J. W. (1984). Heterosexual and homosexual patients with acquired immunodeficiency syndrome: A comparison of surveillance, interview, and laboratory data Annals of Internal Medicine, 100, 213-218.

Gunther, G. (1985). Constitutional Law, (11th ed.). New York: Warner Books.

Guthrie, J. W. (1981). Emerging politics of educational policy Education Evaluation & Policy Analysis, 3, 75-82

Guthrie, J. W., & Reed, R. J. (1986) Educational administration and policy: Effective leadership for American education. Englewood Cliffs, NJ: Prentice-Hall.

Hammett, L. (1986). Protecting children with AIDS against arbitrary exclusion from school. California Law Review, 74, 1373-1407.

Hardy, Jr., W. D. (1981). Feline leukemia virus and non-Aneoplastic diseases. Journal of American Animal Hospital Association, 17, 941.

Hardy, R., Allen, D., & Morgan, E. (1985). The incidence rate of acquired immunodeficiency syndrome in selected populations. Journal of the American Medical Association, 253, 215.

Harmon, M. M. (1969, September). Administration policy formulation and the public interest. Public Administration Review, 29, 483-491.

Harness, W. (1986). AIDS: An emerging crises. Labor Law Journal, 37, 559-563.

Harris, C., Butkus-Small, C. B., Klein, R. S., Friedland, G. H., Moll, B., Emeson, E. E., Spigland, I., & Steigbigel, N. H. (1983). Immunodeficiency in female sexual partners of men with the acquired immunodeficiency syndrome. New England Journal of Medicine, 308, 1181-1184.

Haseltine, W. A. (1986). The slow insidious nature of the HTLV's. ASM News, 52, 3.

Haseltine, W. A. & Wong-Staal, F. (1988, October). The molecular biology of the AIDS virus. Scientific American. pp. 52-62

Heaney, G. J. (1986). The constitutional rights of informational privacy: Does it protect children suffering from AIDS? Fordham Urban Law Journal, 14, 927-969.

Heckler, M. M. (1985). The challenge of acquired immunodeficiency syndrome. Annals of Internal Medicine, 103, 655-656.

Henderson, D. K., Saah, A. J., Zak, B. J., Kaslow, R. A., Lane, H. C., Folks, T., Blackwelder, W. C., Schmitt, J., Lacamera, D. J., Masur, H., & Fauci A. S. (1986). Risk of nosocomial infection with human T-cell lymphotropic virus type III/lymphadenopathy-associated virus in a large cohort of intensively exposed health care workers. Annals of Internal Medicine, 104, 644-647.

Henle, W., Henle, G., & Lennette, E. T. (1979, July). The Epstein-Barr virus. Scientific American. pp. 90-92.

Heyward, W. L., & Curran, J. W. (1988, October). The epidemiology of AIDS in the U.S. Scientific American. pp. 72-81.

Hirsch, M. S., Wormser, G. P., Schooley, R. T., Ho, D. D., Felenstein, D., Hopkins, C. C., Joline, C., Duncanson, F., Sarngaharan, M. G., Saxinger, C., & Gallo, R. C. (1985). Risk of nosocomial infection with human T-cell lymphotropic virus type III (HTLV-III). New England Journal of Medicine, 312, 1-4.

Ho, D. D., Byington, R. E., Schooley, R. T., Flynn, T., Rota, T. R., & Hirsch, M. S. (1985). Infrequency of isolation of HTLV-III virus from saliva in AIDS. New England Journal of Medicine, 313, 1606.

Ho, D. D., Rota, T. R., Schooley, R. T., Kaplan, R. C., Allan, J. D., Groopman, J. E., Resnick, L., Felenstein, D., Andrews, C. A., & Hirsch, M. S. (1985). Isolation of HTLV-III from cerebrospinal fluid and neural tissues of patients with neurologic syndromes related to the acquired immunodeficiency syndrome. New England Journal of Medicine, 313, 1493-1497.

Ho, D. D., Schooley, R. T., Rota, T. R., Kaplan, J. C., Flynn, T., Salahuddin, S. Z., Gonda, M. A., & Hirsch, M. S. (1984). HTLV-III in the semen and blood of a healthy homosexual man. Science, 226, 451-453.

Horowitz, R., & Darris, A. (1986). Special report: Pediatric AIDS; emerging policies. Children's Legal Rights Journal, 7, 1-25.

Immunization levels inch up, but "conquered diseases" remain threat. (1975). Medical World News. p. 86.

Intergovernmental Health Policy Project. (1987). A summary of AIDS law from the 1986 legislative sessions. George Washington University, Washington, D. C. pp. 4-25.

Jaffe, J. W., Feorino, P. M., Darrow W.W., O'Malley, P. M., Getchell, J. P., Warfield, D. T., Jones, B. M., Echenberg, D. F., Francis, D. P., & Curran, J. W. (1985). Persistent infection with human T-lymphotropic virus type III/ lymphadenopathy-associated virus in apparently healthy homosexual men. Annals of Internal Medicine, 102, 627-631.

Jason, J. M., McDougal, S., Dixon, G., Lawrence, D. N., Kennedy, M. S., Hilgartner, M., Aledort, L., & Evatt, B. L. (1986). HTLVIII/LAV antibody & immune status of household contacts & sexual partners of persons with hemophilia. Journal of the American Medical Association, 255, 212-215.

Johnson, Jr., H. C. (1975). Educational policy study and the historical perspective. Educational Administration Quarterly, 11, 38-54.

Jones, N. L. (1986). The education for all handicapped children act: Coverage of children with acquired immune deficiency syndrome (AIDS). Journal of Law & Education, 15, 195-206.

Kanki, P. J., Alroy, J., & Essex, M. (1985). Isolation of T-lymphotropic retrovirus related to HTLV-III/LAV from wild-caught African green monkeys. Science, 230, 951-954.

Kanki, P. J., Kurth, R., Becker, W., Dreesman, G., McLane, M. F., & Essex, M. (1985). Antibodies to simian T-lymphotropic retrovirus type III in African green monkeys and recognition of STLV-III viral proteins by AIDS and related sera. Lancet, 1, 1330-1331.

Kanki, P. J., McLane, M. F., King, Jr., M. W., Letvin, N. L., Hunt, R. D., Sehgal, P., Daniel, M. D., Desrosiers, R. C., & Essex, M. (1985). Serologic identification & characterization of a macaque T-lymphotropic retrovirus closely related to HTLV-III. Science, 228, 1199-1201.

Kaplan, J. E., Oleskc, J. M., Gretchell, J. P., Kalyanaraman, V. S., Minnefor, A. B., Zabala-Ablan, M., Joshi, V., Denny, T., Cabradilla, C. D., Rogers, M. F., et al. (1985). Evidence against transmission of human T- lymphotropic virus/lymph-Aadenopathy-associated virus (HTLV-III/LAV) in families of children with the acquired immunodeficiency syndrome. Petiatric Infectious Diseascs, 4, 468-471.

Kaplan, J. E. (1986, February). A modern-day plague. Natural History. pp. 28-33.

Keough, K. E. & Seaton, G. (1988). Superintendents' views on AIDS: A national survey. Phi Delta Kappan, 2, 358- 361.

Kestens, L., Melbye, M, Biggar, R. J., Stevens, W. J., Piot, P., DeMuynck, A., Taelman, H., Defeyter, M., Paluku, L., & Gigase, P. L. (1985). Endemic African Kaposi's sarcoma is not associated with immunodeficiency. International Journal of Cancer, 36, 49-54.

Koop, C. E. (1987). Surgeon General's Report on AIDS. Public Health Reports, 102, 1-3.

Kreiss, J. K., Kitchen, L. W., Prince, H. E., Kasper, C. K., & Essex, M. (1985). Antibody to human T-lymphotropic virus type III in wives of hemophiliacs: Evidence for heterosexual transmission. Annals of Internal Medicine, 102, 623-626.

Kreiss, J. K., Kocch, D., Plummer, F. A., Holmes, K. K., Lightfoote, M., Piot, P., Ronald, A., Ndinya-Achola, J. O., D'Costa, L. J., Roberts, P., Ngugi, E. N., & Quinn, T. C. (1986). AIDS virus infection in Nairobi prostitutes. New England Journal of Medicine, 314, 414-418.

Krieger, L. (1985, August). Federal agencies report new tests to screen AIDS from blood supply. American Medical News. p. 11.

Kube, L. Y. (1986). AIDS and employment discrimination under the federal rchabilitation act of 1973 and Virginia's rights of persons with disabilities act. University of Richmond Law Review, 20, 425-449.

Landsman, S. H., Ginzburg, H. M., & Weiss, S. H. (1985). The AIDS epidemic. New England Journal of Medicine, 312, 521.

Langer, W. L. (1964). The black death. Science. 210, 114- 121.

Langone, J. (1985, December). AIDS. Discover. pp. 28-53.

Langone, J. (1986, September). AIDS Update: Still no reason for hysteria. Discover. pp. 28-47.

Lapointe, N., Michand, J., Pekovic, D., Chausseau, J., & Dupuy, J. M. (1985). Transplacental transmission of HTLV- III virus. New England Journal of Medicine, 312, 1325- 1326.

Leishman, K. (1987, September). AIDS and insects. Atlantic. pp. 56-72.

Leonard, A. S. (1985). Employment discrimination against persons with AIDS. University of Dayton Law Review, 10, 681-696.

Leonard, A. S. (1987). AIDS in the workplace. In H. L. Dalton & S. Burris, AIDS and the Law, A Guide for the Public (pp. 109-125). New Haven: Yale University Press.

Levy, J., Hollander, M., Shimabukuro, J., Mills, J., & Kaminsky, L. (1985). Isolation of AIDS-Associated retroviruses from the cerebrospinal fluid and brain of patients with neurological symptoms. Lancet, 2, 586-588.

Levy, J., Kaminsky, L. Morrow, J., Steimer, K., Luciw, P., Dina, D., Hoxie, J., & Oshiro, L. (1985). Infection by the retrovirus associated with acquired immune deficiency syndrome. Annals of Internal Medicine, 103, 694-699.

Levy, J., Pan, L., Beth-Giraldo, E., Kaminsky, L., Henle, G., Henle, W., & Giraldo, G. (1986). Abscence of antibodies to the human immunodeficiency virus in serum from Africa prior to 1975. National Academy of Science, 83, 7935-7937.

Lewis, H. E. (1987). Acquired immunodeficiency syndrome: State legislative activity. Journal of American Medical Association, 258, 2410-2414.

Lieberman, A., & McLaughlin, M. W. (Eds.). (1982). Policy making in education. Chicago, IL: Chicago Press.

Lindblom, C. E. (1968). The policy-making process. Engelwood Cliffs, NJ: Prentice-Hall.

Lui, K. J., Lawrence. D. N., Meade, M., Morgan, W., Peterman, T. A., Haverkos, H. W., & Bregman, D. J. (1986). A model-based approach for estimating mean incubation period of transfusion-associated acquired immunodeficiency syndrome. Annals of Internal Medicine, 83, 3051- 3155.

Lyden, F. J., Shipman, G., & Wilkinson, R. J. (1968). Decision flow analysis: A methodology for studying the policy-making process. In P. Le Breton, Comparative Administrative Theory (pp. 155-156). Seattle: University of Washington Press.

Lyons, S. F., Jupp, P. G., & Schoub, B. D. (1986). Survival of HIV in the common bedbug. Lancet, 2, 45.

Macher, A. (1988). The pathology of AIDS. Public Health Reports, 103, 246-254.

MacLeod, C. (1987, October). Comments made while participating in an AIDS panel discussion at the National Science Teacher's Association Convention, Miami Beach, FL.

Mann, J. M., Quinn, T. C., Francis, H., Nzilambi, N., Bosenge, N., Bila, K., McCormick, J. B., Ruti, K., Asila, P. K., & Curran, J. W. (1986). The prevalence of HTLV- III/LAV in household contacts of patients with confirmed AIDS & controls in Kinshasa, Zaire. Journal of the American Medical Association, 256, 721-724.

Marion, R. W., Wiznia, A. A., Hutcheon, R. G., & Rubenstein, A. (1986). Human T-cell lymphotropic virus type III (HTLV-III) embryopathy: A new dysmorphic syndrome associated with intrauterine HTLV-III infection. American Journal of Disease in Children, 140, 638-640.

Martin, L. S., McDougal, J. S., & Loskoski, S. L. (1985). Disinfection and inactivation of the T-lymphotropic virus type-III/lymphadenopathy-associated virus. Journal of Infectious Diseases, 152, 400-403.

Marx, J. L. (1982). Cancer cell genes linked to viral onc genes. Science, 216, 724.

Matthews, T. J., & Bolognesi, D. P. (1988, October). AIDS vaccines. Scientific American. pp. 120-127.

McCormick, K. (1986, May). Sound policies and expert advice are your best protection against AIDS. American School Board Journal. pp. 36-37.

McCray, E. (1986). The cooperative needlestick surveillance group: Occupational risk of the acquired immunodeficiency syndrome among health care workers. New England Journal of Medicine, 314, 1127-1132.

McNeill, W. H. (1976). Plaques and people. New York: Anchor.

Message from Secretary Heckler and letter from Commissioner Young. (1985). FDA Drug Bulletin, 15, 26.

Michealis, B. A. & Levy, J. A. (1987). Recovery of the human immunodeficiency virus from serum. Journal of American Medical Association, 257, 1327.

Montagnier, L. (1985). Lymphadenopathy-associated virus from molecular biology to pathogenicity. Annals of Internal Medicine, 103, 689-693.

Morgan, W. M. & Curran, J. W. (1986). Acquired immunodeficiency syndrome: Current and future trends. Public Health Reports, 101, 459-465.

Morgenstern, M. S. (1978). The role of the federal government in protecting citizens from communicable diseases. University of Cincinnati Law Review, 47, 537-560.

Nahmias, A. J., Weiss, J., Yaa, X., Lee, F., Kodsi, R., Schanfield, M., Matthews, T., Bolognesi, D., Durack, D., Motulsky, A., Kanki, P., & Essex, M. (1986). Evidence for human infection with an HTLV-III/LAV-like virus in central Africa, 1959. Lancet, 2, 1279-1280.

Nanula, P. J. (1987). Protecting confidentiality in the effort to control AIDS. Harvard Journal on Legislation, 24, 315-349.

National Education Association. (1986). Recommended guidelines for dealing with AIDS in the schools. Journal of School Health, 56, 129-130.

National Gay Rights Advocates. (1986, September). AIDS and handicap discrimination: A survey of 50 states and the District of Columbia. San Francisco, CA: Author.

Nichols, C. D. (1984). AIDS - A new reason to regulate homosexuality? Journal of Contemporary Law, 11, 315-343.

Norman, C. (1985a). Africa and the origin of AIDS. Science, 230, 1141.

Norman, C. (1985b). AIDS virus presents moving target. Science, 230, 1357.

Osborne, J. E. (1987). The AIDS epeidemic: Discovery of a new disease. In H.L. Dalton & S. Burris (Eds.), AIDS and the law, A guide for the public (pp. 17-27). New Haven: Yale University Press.

Pahwa, S., Kaplan, M., Fikrig, S., Popovic, M., Sarngadharan, A., & Pahwa, R. (1986). Spectrum of human T-cell lymphotropic virus type III infection in children. Journal of the American Medical Association, 255, 2299.

Pape, J. W., Liautaud, B., Thomas, F., Mathurin, J. R., St. Amand, M. A., Boncy, M., Pean, V., Pamphile, M., Laroche, C., Dehovitz, J., & Johnson, W. D. (1985). The acquired immunodeficiency syndrome in Haiti. Annals of Internal Medicine, 103, 674-678.

Parmet, L. (1985). AIDS and quarantine: The revival of an archaic doctrine. Hofstra Law Review, 14, 76-77.

Partida, G. A. (1986). AIDS: Do children with AIDS have a right to attend school? Pepperdine Law Review, 13, 1041-A1061.

Perisco. (1976). The great swine flu epidemic of 1918. American Heritage, 27, 28-32.

Peterman, T. A., Stoneburner, R. L., & Allen, J. R. (1986, June). Risk of HTLV-III/LAV transmission to household contacts of persons with transfusion associated HTLV/LAV infection. Paper presented at the Second International Conference on Acquired Immune Deficiency Syndrome (AIDS), Paris, France.

Peterson, L. J. (1986). Educational policy making and interpretation: A bibliography. Monticello, IL: Vance Bibliographies.

Peterson, L. J., Rossmiller, R. A., & Volz, M. M. (1978). The law and public school operation (2nd ed.). New York: Harper & Row.

Petricciani, J. C., (1985). Licensed tests for antibody to human T-lymphotropic virus type III: Sensitivity and specificity. Annals of Internal Medicine, 103, 726-729.

Petteway. (1944). Compulsory quarantine and treatment of persons with venereal disease. Florida Law Journal, 18, 13.

Poiesz, B. J., Ruscetti, F. W., Gazdar, A. F., Bunn, P. A., Minna, J. D., & Gallo, R. C. (1980). Detection and Isolation of type C retrovirus particles from fresh and cultured lymphocytes of a patient with cutaneous T-cell lymphoma. Medical Science, 77, 7415-7419.

Popovic, M., Sarngadharan, M. G., Reade, M., & Gallo, R. C. (1984). Detection, isolation, and contiuous production of cytopathic retroviruses (HTLV-III) from patients with AIDS and Pre-AIDS. Science, 224, 497-500.

Postell, C. J. (1986). AIDS: A legal, medical, and social problem. Trial, 22, 76-78.

Prentice & Murray. (1984). Liability for transmission of herpes: Using traditional tort principles to encourage honesty in sexual relationships. Journal of Contemporary Law, 11, 67.

Proffitt, M. R. (1988). The AIDS retrovirus. In K.D. Blanchett (ed.), AIDS: A health care management response (pp. 19-30). Rockville, MA: Aspen Publications.

Public Health Service. (1986). Public health service plan for prevention and control of AIDS and the AIDS virus. Public Health Report, 101, 341-348.

Quinn, T. C., Mann, J. M., Curran, J. W., & Piot, P. (1986). AIDS in Africa: An epidemiologic paradigm. Science, 234, 955-963.

Quinn, T. C., Mann, J. M., Curran, J. W., & Piot, P. (1985). Perspectives on the future of AIDS. Journal of the American Medical Association, 253, 247.

Rafferty, K. A., Jr. (1973, October). Herpes viruses and cancer. Scientific American. pp. 26-33.

Reed, S. (1986). AIDS in schools: A special report. Phi Delta Kappan, 67, 4949-498.

Redfield, R. R., & Burke, D. S. (1988, October). HIV infection: The clinical picture. Scientific American. pp. 90-99.

Redfield, R. R., Markham, P. D., Galahuddin, S. Z., Sarngadharan, M. G., Bodner, A. J., Folks, T. M., Ballou, W. R., Wright, D. C., & Gallo, R. C. (1985). Frequent transmission of HTLV-III among spouses of patients with AIDS-related complex & AIDS. Journal of the American Medical Association, 253, 1571-1573.

Rehabilitation Act of 1973. § 504 29 U.S.C. §§ 701-796 (1982), 45 C.F.R. §§ 84 app. A (1985).

Rensberger, B. (1987, October). Mosquitoes and AIDS. Science World. pp. 19-23.

Rogers, M. F. (1985). AIDS in children: A review of the clinical epidemiologic and public health aspects. Pediatric Infectious Diseases, 4, 230-236.

Rohter, L. (1985, September 10). 11,000 boycott classes in AIDS protest. New York Times. p. B-1 & B-5.

Roots of AIDS boycott. (1985, September, 14). New York Times. p. B-1.

Roth & Meisel. (1977). Dangerousness, confidentiality, and the duty to warn. American Journal of Psychiatry, 134, 508-509.

Rothstein, M. A. (1986). Medical screening of workers: Genetics, AIDS, and beyond. The Labor Lawyer, 675-682.

Rothstein, M. A. (1987). Screening workers for AIDS. In H. L. Dalton & S. Burris (Eds.), AIDS and the Law, A Guide for the Public (pp. 126-141). New Haven: Yale University Press.

Rothwell, R. (1951). In D. Lerner & H. D. Lasswell (Eds.), ''Forward'', The Policy Sciences : Recent Developments in Scope and Method (p. ix). Stanford: Stanford University Press.

Rubin, L. (Ed.). (1980). Critical issues in educational policy: an administrator's overview. Boston: Allyn and Bacon.

Sande, M. (1986). Transmission of AIDS: The case against casual contagion. New England Journal of Medicine, 314, 380.

Salahuddin, S., Markham, P., Popovic, M., Sarngadharan, M., Orndorff, S., Fladagar, A., Patec, A., Gold, J., & Gallo, R. (1985). Isolation of infectious human T-cell leukemia/lymphotropic virus type III (HTLV-III) from patients with acquired immunodeficiency syndrome (AIDS) or AIDS-related complex (ARC) and from healthy carriers: As a study of risk groups and tissues sources. Proceedings from the National Academy of Sciences, 82, 5530-5534.

Sarngadharan, M. G., Popovic, M., Bruch, L., Schupach, J., & Gallo, R. C. (1984). Antibodies reactive with human T-lymphotropic retroviruses (HTLV-III) in the serum of patients with AIDS. Science, 224, 506-508.

Saxinger, W. C., Levine, P. H., Dean, A. G., Dethe, G., Lange-Wantzin, G., Moghissi, J., Laurent, F., Hoh, M., Sarngadharan, M. G., & Gallo, R. C. (1985). Evidence for exposure to HTLV-III in Uganda in 1973. Science, 227, 1036-1038.

Schoors, J. B., Berkowitz, A., Cumming, P. P., Katz, A. J., & Sandler, S. G. (1985). Prevalence of HIV antibody in American blood donors. New England Journal of Medicine, 313, 384-385.

Schupach, J., Popovic, M., Gilden, R. V., Gonda, M. A., Sarngadharan, M. G., & Gallo, R. C. (1984). Serological analysis of subgroup of human T-lymphotropic retroviruses (HTLV-III) associated with AIDS. Science, 224, 503-505.

Schwarz, F. A., & Schaffer, F. P. (1985). AIDS in the classroom (Law, Social Policy, and Contagious Disease: A Symposium on AIDS). Hofstra Law Review, 14, 163-191.

Scitovsky, A. A. & Rice, D. P. (1987). Estimating the direct and indirect costs of acquired immunodeficiency syndrome in the United States, 1985, 1986 and 1991. Public Health Reports, 102, 5-17.

Scott, G. B., Fischl, M. A., Klimas, N., Fletcher, M. A., Dickinson, G. M., Levine, R. S., & Parks, W. P. (1985). Mothers of infants with acquired immunodeficiency syndrome: Evidence for both symptomatic & asymptomatic carriers. Journal of the American Medical Association, 253, 363-366.

Seligmann, J., & Gosnell, M. (1984, January). New theories about AIDS: The detective work is frustrating, but researchers are learning more about the nature of the deadly epidemic. Newsweek. pp. 50-51.

Seligmann, J., & Hager, M. (1984, May). Tracing the origin of AIDS. Newsweek. pp. 101-102.

Senak, M. S. (1988). Legal issues facing AIDS patients. In K. D. Blanchet, AIDS: A Health Care Management Response (pp. 99-117). Rockville, Maryland: Aspen Publication.

Shaw, G. M., Harper, M. E., Hahn, B. H., Epstein, L. G., Carleton Gajdusek, D., Price, R. W., Navia, B. A., Petito, R. W., O'Haro, C. J., Groopman, J. E., Cho, E., Oleske, J. M., Wong-Staal. F., & Gallo, R. C. (1985). HTLV-III infection in brains of children and adults with AIDS encephalopathy. Science, 227, 177.

Shumaker, G. M. (1986) AIDS: Does it qualify as a handicap under the rehabilitation act of 1973. Notre Dame Law Review, 61, 572-594.

Sicklick, M. J. (1985). A medical review of AIDS (Law, Social Policy, and Contagious Disease: A Symposium on AIDS). Hofstra Law Review, 14, 5-10.

Silberner, J. (1986, October). No AIDS via mosquitoes. Science News. p. 252.

Silverstein, T. F. (1986) AIDS and employment: An epidemic strikes the workplace and the law. Whittier Law Review, 8, 651-680.

Simmons, R. H., Davis, B. W., Chapman, R. J. K., & Sager, D. D. (1974). Policy flow analysis: A conceptual model for comparative public policy research. Western Political Quarterly, 27, 457-468.

Slaff, J. I., & Brubaker, J. K. (1985). The AIDS epidemic: How you can protect yourself and your family - why you must. New York: Warner Books.

Sodroski, J., Patarca, R., Rosen, C., Wong-Staal, F., & Haseltine, W. (1985). Location of the transactivating region of the genome of the human T-cell lymphotropic virus type III. Science, 227, 74-77.

Sotto, L. J. (1986). Undoing a lesson of fear in the classroom: The legal recourse of AIDS-linked children. University of Pennsylvania Law Review, 135, 193-221.

Speigel, C. (1986). Privacy, sodomy, AIDS and the schools: Case studies in equal protection. Annual Survey of American Law, 221-253.

Spira, T. J., DesJarlais, D. C., Marmor, M., Yancovitz, S., Friedman, S., Garber, J., Cohen, H., Cabradilla, C., & Kalyanaraman, V. C. (1984). Prevalence of antibody to lymphadenopathy-associated virus among drug-detoxification patients in New York [letter]. New England Journal of Medicine, 311, 467-468.

Spire, B., Barre-Sinoussi, E., Montagnieer, L., & Chermann, J. C. (1984). Inactivation of the lymphadenopathy associated virus by chemical disinfectants. Lancet, 1, 899-901.

Stewart, G.J., Cunningham, A. L., Driscoll, G. L., Tyler, J. P. P., Barr, J. A., Gold, J., & Lamont, B. J. (1985). Transmission of human T-cell lymphotropic virus type III (HTLV-III) by artificial insemination by donor. Lancet, 2, 581-584.

Swenson, R. M. (1988). Plagues, history, and AIDS. The American Scholar, 57, 183-200.

Tarr, A. (1985, November 25). AIDS: The legal issue widen. National Law Journal. p. 28.

Temin, H. M. (1972, January). RNA directed DNA synthesis. Scientific American. pp. 24-33.

Thiry, L., Sprecher-Goldberger, S., Jonckheer, T., Levy, J., Van De-Perre, P., Henrivaux, P., Cogniaux-Leclerc, J., & Clumeck, N. (1985). Isolation of AIDS virus from cell-free breast milk of three healthy virus carriers. Lancet, 2, 891-892.

Thomas, C. L. (Ed). (1985). Taber's Cyclopedia, Medical Edition (15th ed.). Philadelphia: Davis.

Thomas, P. A., Jaffe, H. W., Spira, T. J., Reiss, R., Guerrero, I. C., & Auerbach, D. (1984). Unexplained immunodeficiency in children: A surveillance report. Journal of the American Medical Association, 252, 639-644.

Thomas, P. A., Lubin, K., Enlow, R. W., & Getchell, J. (1985, April). Comparison of HTLV-III serology. T-cell levels and general health status of children whose mothers have AIDS with children of healthy inner-city mothers in New York. Paper presented at the First International Conference on AIDS, Atlanta, GE.

Titus, D. L. (1986). AIDS as a handicap under the federal rehabilitation act of 1973. Washington & Lee Law Review, 43, 1515-1535.

Tribe, L. (1978). American Constitutional Law. New York: Warner Books.

Turner, J. G. & Williamson, K. M. (1986). AIDS: A challenge for contemporary nursing, Part I. Focus on Critical Care, 13, 53-61.

U.S. Department of Health & Human Services. (1985-1986). State Immunization Requirements.

Varmus, H., (1987, September). Reverse transcriptase. Scientific American. pp. 56-64.

Villee, C. A., Solomon, E. P., & Davis, P. W. (1985) Biology. Philadelphia: Saunders.

Vogt, M. W., Craven, D. E., Crawford, D. F., Witt, D. J., Byington, R., Schooley, R. T., & Hirsch, M. S. (1986). Isolation of HTLV-III/LAV from cervical secretions of women at risk of AIDS. Lancet, 1. 525-527.

Wade, L. L. & Curry, R. J. (1970). A logic of public policy: Aspects of political economy. Belmont California: Wadsworth.

Weber, J. N., & Weiss, R. A. (1988, October). HIV infection: The cellular picture. Scientific American. pp. 100-109.

Weiss, R. A. (1987). AIDS vaccine: Research on target. Science News, 131, 84.

Weiss, S. H., Saxinger, C., Rechtman, D., Grieco, M. H., Nadler, J., Holman, S., Ginzgurg, H. M., Groopman, J. E., Goedert, J. J., Markham, P. D., Gallo, R. C., Blattner, W. A., & Landsman, S. (1985). HTLV-III infection among health care workers: Association with needlestick injuries. Journal of the American Medical Association, 254, 2089-2093.

Welker, M. J. (1986). The impact of AIDS upon public schools: A problem of jurisprudence. West's Education Law Reporter, 32, 603-617.

Whiteside, M. E., Withum, D., Tavris, D., & MacLeod, C. (April, 1985). Outbreak of nonidentifiable-risk acquired immunodeficiency syndrome (AIDS) in Belle Glade, Florida. Paper presented at the First International Conference on AIDS, Atlanta, GE.

Wiley, C., Schrier, R., Nelson, J., Lamport, P., & Oldstone, M. (1986). Cellular localization of human immunodeficiency virus infection within the brains of acquired immunodeficiency syndrome patients. National Academy of Science, 83, 7089-7093.

Wofsy, C. B., Hauer, L. B., Michaelis, B. A., Cohen, J. B., Padian, N. S., Evans, L. A., & Levy, J. A. (1986). Isolation of AIDS-associated retrovirus from genital secretion of women with antibodies to the virus. Lancet, 1, 527-529.

Wong-Staal, F. (1986). Comment. Science, 231, 451.

Wong-Staal, F., Shaw, G. M., Hahn, B. H., Salahuddin, S. Z., Popovic, M., Markham, P., Redfield, R., & Gallo, R. C. (1985). Genomic diversity of human T-lymphotropic virus type III (HTLV-III). Science, 229, 759-762.

Yankauer, A. (1988). AIDS and public health. American Journal of Public Health, 78, 364-365.

Yarchoan, R., Mitsuya, H., & Broder, S. (1988, October). AIDS therapies. Scientific American. pp. 110-119.

Yudof, M. G., Kirp, D. L., van Geel, T., & Levin, B. (1982). Educational policy and the law; cases and materials. Berkley, CA: McCutchan Publishing.

Zagury, D., Bernard, J., Leibowitch, J., Safari, B., Groopman, J. E., Feldman, M., Sarngadharan, M. G., & Gallo, R. C. (1984). HTLV-III in cells cultured from semen of two patients. Science, 226, 449-451.

Zeigler, J. B., Cooper, D. A., Johnson, R. D., & Gold, J. (1985). Postnatal transmission of AIDS associated retro-virus from mother to infant. Lancet, 1, 896-898.

Ziza, J. M., Brun-Vezinet, F., Venet, A., Rouzioux, C. H., Traversat, J., Israel-Biet, B., Barre-Sinoussi, F., Chermann, J. C., & Godeau, P. (1985). Lymphadenopathy-associated virus isolated from bronchoalveolar lavage fluid in AIDS-related complex with lymphoid interstitial pneumonitis. New England Journal of Medicine, 313, 183.

Zuckerman, A. J. (1986) AIDS and insects. British Medical Journal, 292, 1094-1095.

GLOSSARY

AIDS (Acquired Immunodeficiency Syndrome) - An acquired illness of the immune system which reduces the body's ability to fight certain types of infection and cancers.

AIDS-associated Retrovirus (ARV) - The name given to a retrovirus recovered from AIDS patients. Further investigation revealed that ARV and HTLV-III were different names for the same virus.

AIDS Dementia - A degenerative disorder of the brain and central nervous system caused by the human immunodeficiency virus (HIV) that leads to progressive deterioration of mental and neurological processes.

Antibody - A special protein manufactured by the body's immune system in response to specific foreign agents.

Antigen - A substance that stimulates the production of antibodies.

Appeal - A request made to a higher court to review the actions of a lower court in order to correct mistakes or injustice.

ARC (AIDS Related Complex) - A group of symptoms and illnesses manifested by a person with an impaired immune system.

Asymptomatic - A person who demonstrates no subjective or objective signs of illness.

Case Law - A body of law that has been created by judicial decisions. Case law provides a primary source of legal authority.

Common Law - A system of law in which authority is not derived expressly from statutes; rather, traditional legal principles are derived from usage and custom as enunciated by court decisions.

Compelling State Interest - A reason underlying a law, rule, policy or action that is strong enough to justify the limitation of individual constitutional or federal statutory rights.

Contagious Disease - An illness caused by a specific infectious agent, such as a virus, bacteria, or fungus, that is transmitted, directly or indirectly, from an infected carrier to a susceptible host

Deoxyribonucleic Acid (DNA) - A class of nucleic acids characterized by the presence of the sugar deoxyribose and the pyrimidine thymine. Molecular DNA consists of two complementary strands of nucleotides wound in a double helix. The DNA molecule is an essential component of all life and constitutes the basic chromosomal material transmitting the hereditary pattern.

Dictum (orbiter dictum) - A digression; an opinion expressed by a judge in a proceeding that is unrelated to the decision rendered by the court.

Due Process of Law - Implies that the powers of the government are exercised fairly and equitably in order to protect the rights of citizens as guaranteed by the fifth and fourteenth amendments.

ELISA Test (Enzyme-Linked Immunosorbent Assay) - An efficient biochemical test used to measure the presence of HIV antibodies within human blood.

Epidemic - The appearance of an illness or disease that attacks many people at the same time within the same geographical area.

Epidemiology - The science concerned with defining and explaining the interrelationship of factors that determine disease frequency and distribution.

Ex Parte - With only one side present; *ex parte* judicial proceedings involve only one party without notice to, or contestation by, any person adversely affected.

Ex Rel. - On behalf of; *ex rel.* designates a private individual on whose behalf the state is acting in a legal case.

Exposure - When an individual has made direct or indirect contact with an infectious agent.

False Negative - When the test results from an infected person fail to indicate the presence of the disease or condition.

False Positive - When the test results from a non-infected person indicate the presence of disease or condition.

Finding - A conclusion of a court or jury regarding a question of fact.

Fundamental Rights - Rights that are founded upon the express terms of the Constitution or may be implied from those terms. Life, liberty and property are included among these rights.

Hearing - A judicial examination of factual or legal issues; an oral proceeding before a court or quasi-judicial tribunal.

High Risk Group - Persons who have characteristics or behaviors that increase their chances of acquiring an infection.

Holding - The rule of law in a legal case; that part of the judicial opinion that applies the law to the facts of the case.

Human Immunodeficiency Virus (HIV) - A specific retrovirus that has been identified as capable of destroying the human immune system making it susceptible to life-threatening opportunistic infections or rare cancers. The human immunodeficiency virus is a member of a large family of viruses called retroviridae, which have the unique ability to manufacture DNA from RNA using a specialized enzyme called reverse transcriptase.

Human T-cell Lymphotropic Virus type III (HTLV-III) - A name given to a specific retrovirus whose host target is a specialized white blood cell known as a T4 lymphocyte, which functions within the human immune system to defend the body against disease. Prior to 1986, HTLV-III was used to identify the various isolates (e.g., LAV, ARV) that were associated with AIDS. This designation has since been replaced by HIV.

Immune System - A complex network of organs and cells that enables the body to defend itself against infections and substances which are foreign to the body.

Incidence - The number of new case of a disease or condition over a specific period of time.

Infectious Disease - An illness that results from the entry, development or multiplication of a pathogenic organism.

Injunction - A court order that may be used to either require some action or prohibit some action on the part of an individual or organization.

Intermediate Scrutiny - One of three standards of review available to the judiciary under an equal protection analysis. Under intermediate scrutiny, the disputed classification must exhibit a substantial relationship to the achievement of an important governmental interest. Traditionally, intermediate scrutiny has been used to analyze classifications involving women.

Lymphadenopathy-associated Virus (LAV) - The name given to a retrovirus recovered from persons with lymphadenopathy or enlarged lymph nodes who were also at high risk for AIDS. Further investigation revealed that LAV and HTLV-III were different names for the same retrovirus.

Latency Period - The time between the contraction of a disease and the clinical manifestation of the disease.

Minimum Scrutiny - See rational basis test.

Mutation - A change in the genetic structure of a cell that can alter the production or operation of proteins within the cell.

Opportunistic Infections - A variety of diseases that occur due to the opportunity afforded by the altered physiological state of the host.

Pediatric AIDS - A population group involving children under the age of 13 years with clinical AIDS.

Precedent - A court decision involving a question of law that gives authority or direction on how to decide a similar question of law in a later case under similar circumstances.

Prevalence - The number of cases of disease present in a specific population at a specific time.

Rational Basis Test - One of three standards of review available to the judiciary under an equal protection analysis. The rational basis test or minimum scrutiny requires that a classification must be rationally related to the achievement of a legitimate state interest. This test is usually employed when no fundamental interest is involved and the burden of proof rests with the complainant.

Ribonucleic Acid (RNA) - A class of nucleic acids characterized by the presence of the sugar ribose and the pyrimidine uracil. Molecular RNA is important in cellular protein synthesis.

Relief - Legal redress or assistance sought in a court of law.

Remand - To send back; appellate court decisions may require that a case return to the court where the case began for further proceedings.

Retrovirus - A special group of viruses that can manufacture deoxyribonucleic acid (DNA) from ribonucleic acid (RNA) and are capable of causing disease in a variety of plants and animals. Retroviruses are associated with many human diseases, including cancer and AIDS.

Reverse Transcriptase - An enzyme that is unique to retroviruses which enables them to manufacture DNA from RNA and undergo replication.

Risk Factors - Any personal characteristic or behavior that increases the likelihood that a person will be affected by a specific condition or disease.

Screening - The process of identifying undetected disease by using tests, examinations or other procedures.

Sensitivity - The ability of a screening test to correctly identify persons with a specific condition or disease.

Seroconversion - The development of serological evidence of antibody response to a disease or vaccine or when the serological status of blood changes from seronegative to seropositive.

Seronegative - The serological status of blood when it is tested and the results cannot confirm the presence of specific disease antibodies.

Seropositive - The serological status of blood when it is tested and the results confirm the presence of specific disease antibodies.

Statute - An established rule or law; an act of the state or federal legislature.

Strict Scrutiny - A legal test that is often employed to measure classification against the equal protection clause of the fourteenth amendment when a fundamental interest or suspect classification is involved. Under this judicial standard, the state bears the burden of proving that its actions are motivated by a compelling interest and the distinctions that are created by the law are necessary to further its purpose.

Suspect Class - Persons whose equal protection rights may be denied because they belong to a specific class, such as alienage, indigency, illegitimacy, national origin or race.

Surveillance - The process of collecting, analyzing, and interpreting public health data as it relates to disease.

T-Lymphocyte (T-Cell) - A type of white blood cell that is essential to the human immune system in its fight against infection and disease.

Transmission - The transfer of a disease from one person to another person.

Vaccine - A suspension of infectious agents or some component of them that is given for the purpose of establishing resistance to an infectious disease.

Virus - A submicroscopic parasite that is dependent upon on nutrients within a cell for its metabolic and reproductive needs.

Western Blot - A highly sensitive serological test that is able to quantify the presence of antibodies to viral proteins within human blood.

APPENDIX

Contemporary Legal Cases Involving Acquired Immunodeficiency Syndrome

Cases Decided in 1990

Wilson v. Reno County. Dismissing a 42 U.S.C. § 1983 claim brought forth by a nurse who alleged she was fired because she refused to provide home care to a patient inflicted with AIDS.

Doe v. Meachum. Granting a judgment of consent concerning the institution of an appropriate AIDS policy and educational program for prison officials and inmates.

Doe v. State of Fla. Judicial Qualifications Comm'n. Granting an injunction to prevent enforcement of the confidentiality provision of Art. V, § 12(d) of the Florida Constitution.

Deutsch v. Federal Bureau of Prisons. Dismissing an Eighth Amendment claim brought forth by a prison inmate because he was forced to share a prison cell with an inmate diagnosed as HIV sero-positive.

Coleman v. American Red Cross. Denying a motion to compel blood banking officials to disclose confidential information concerning blood donors.

Cain v. Hyatt Legal Services. Holding that the Pennsylvania Human Relations Act prevents discrimination against employees with AIDS.

Doe v. Borough of Barrington and Runnemede. Dismissing a 42 U.S.C. § 1983 right to privacy claim brought forth by a person with AIDS.

Cases Decided in 1989

Gay Men's Health Crisis and the N.Y. State Dep't of Health v. Secretary of Health and Human Serv. and the U.S. Centers for Disease Control. Granting a motion for declaratory and injunctive relief involving the constitutionality of statutory and agency restrictions on federally-funded AIDS education materials and activities.

Movie & Video World, Inc. v. Board of County Commissioners of Palm Beach County, Fla. Upholding the constitutionality of a county ordinance requiring the removal of viewing booth doors in adult bookstores.

Planned Parenthood of Southern Nevada, Inc. v. Clark County School Dist. Affirming a district court's decision dismissing a first amendment claim brought forth by Planned Parenthood against the school district for refusing to allow them to publish advertisements in school-sponsored publications.

Doe v. Attorney Gen. of the United States. Dismissing a right to privacy claim brought forth under the due process clause of the Fifth Amendment by a person with AIDS.

Feigley v. Fulcomer. Dismissal of Eighth Amendment prisoner claim alleging failure of prison officials to protect prisoners from AIDS.

Hayley v. Evans. Dismissing a constitutional claim brought forth by HIV positive prisoners alleging they were denied access to experimental and/or novel forms of medical treatment for their children from a private physician.

Doe v. American Red Cross Blood Serv. Dismissing a strict liability claim involving the transfusion of blood products contaminated with the AIDS virus.

Christopher v. Barry. Dismissing a fifth amendment and 42 U.S.C. § 1983 claim brought forth by the parents of a child sero-positive for HIV.

Holt *et al.* v. Norris. Affirming a district court's dismissal of a fifth amendment and 42 U.S.C. § 1983 claim brought forth by prison inmates asserting failure on the part of prison officials to protect the general prison population for AIDS.

Child v. School Bd. of Fairfax County, Va. Reversing a district court's award of attorney's fees and costs to the parents of a child with AIDS.

Cases Decided in 1988

Brown v. Owens. Dismissing the constitutional claims of an AIDS-conscious prisoner seeking an injunction against prison officials to prevent the housing of additional prisoners with AIDS.

Doe v. Centinela Hosp. Granting a motion to admit a HIV sero-positive patient to a residential school and drug rehabilitation program under § 504 of the Rehabilitation Act.

Doe v. City of Minneapolis. Upholding the constitutionality of a Minneapolis city ordinance requiring the removal of viewing booth doors in adult bookstore.

Doe v. Dolton Elementary School Dist. No. 148. Granting a motion for a preliminary injunction to return a student with AIDS to his regular classes as a full-time student.

Doe v. Travenol Laboratories, Inc. Granting a motion to dismiss strict liability and breach of warranty claims involving blood products contaminated with AIDS virus on the grounds that Minnesota law insulates the suppliers of blood products for such claims.

Glick v. Henderson. Dismissal of a 42 U.S.C. § 1983 prisoner claim alleging failure and refusal of prison officials to protect prisoners from AIDS.

Glover v. Eastern Nebraska Community Office of Retardation. Overturning a Nebraska Human Services Agency (ENHSA) policy that subjects employees to mandatory blood testing on 14th amendment grounds.

Graves v. Blue Cross of Cal. Granting a motion to remand a case involving an AIDS disability claim against Blue Cross of California. The court concluding that the federal Employee Retirement Income Security Act of 1974 ("ERISA") does not pre-empt claims brought pursuant to section 790.03(h) of the California Insurance Code.

Jezick v. Frame. Dismissing a 42 U.S.C. § 1983 claim brought forth by a prisoner who claims that his constitutional rights have been violated because he had been housed with persons who have AIDS.

Kirkendall v. Harbor Insur. Co. Dismissing a strict liability claim involving the transfusion of blood products contaminated with AIDS virus.

Kozup v. Georgetown Univ. Refusal to hold medical facility and blood bank strictly liable for AIDS-related death brought upon by contaminated blood product.

Lewis v. Prison Health Serv., Inc. Dismissing constitutional claims of a HIV-positive prisoner administratively segregated from the general prison population.

Logrande v. Local 851 Employer Group Pension Plan. Denying a motion to suspend the retirement benefits of a truck driver who returned to work to help defray the medical expenses of his son who was diagnosed as having AIDS.

Mason v. Regional Medical Center of Hopkins County. Concluding that the claim of constitutionality protected blood donor privacy is a claim beyond the boundaries of the right of privacy as previous established by the Supreme Court.

Morales v. Vasiliadis. Dismissing a U.S.C. § 1983 civil rights action against a public defender who allegedly disclosed in court that his client had contracted AIDS.

Muhammad v. Carlson. Dismissing a due process claim of an AIDS prisoner segregated from general prison population.

People v. Alpha Therapeutic Corp. Granting a motion to dismiss strict liability and breach of warranty claims involving blood products contaminated with AIDS virus.

Roe v. Fauver. Dismissing a constitutional claim brought forth by a female prisoner with AIDS who was confined to a hospital room during the construction of a facility to house female prisoners suffering from AIDS.

Suburban Video v. City of Delafield. Granting a permanent injunction declaring a Delafield ordinance regulating "adult-oriented establishments" unconstitutional.

United States v. Moore. Denying motions for acquittal and a new trial following two assault convictions on the basis that there was insufficient evidence to prove that the mouth and teeth constitute a deadly and dangerous weapon capable of transmitting AIDS.

Cases Decided in 1987

School Bd. of Nassau County v. Arline. Holding that a person afflicted with the contagious disease of tuberculosis may be considered a handicapped individual within the meaning of § 540 of the Rehabilitation Act.

Berg v. The Health & Hosp. Corp. of Marion County. Sustaining an ordinance regulating commercial premises conducive to the spread of communicable diseases on the substantial government interest in preventing the spread of AIDS.

Brown v. Delaware County Prison. Dismissing 42 U.S.C. § 1983 claim of prisoner confined with persons known to be infected with the AIDS virus.

Chalk v. United States. Reversing a district court decision to uphold a § 504 claim presented by an Orange County exceptional education teacher diagnosed as having AIDS.

Coffee v. Cutter Biological. Upholding a Connecticut "blood shield" statute which bars product liability claims involving manufactured blood components.

Davis v. Stanley. Refusing to hold local police department strictly liable for not administering AIDS blood test to suspects prior to incarceration.

Doe v. Belleville Pub. School Dist. No. 118. Denying a motion to dismiss an Educational for All Handicapped Act claim of a child with HIV sero-positivity.

Institut Pasteur v. United States. Reversing claims court dismissal of a contract action involving AIDS-related patent.

Jarrett v. Faulkner. Dismissing for lack of specificity, prisoner claim that all inmates undergo AIDS blood testing and that all homosexuals be segregated from the general prison population.

Judd v. Packard. Dismissing constitutional claims of prisoner who tested positively for the presence of AIDS virus and thus was segregated from the general prison population.

Kozup v. Georgetown Univ. Refusing to hold health care provider and blood banking center strictly liable for transmission for blood products contaminated with AIDS virus.

Lewis v. Prison Health Serv., Inc. Dismissing 42 U.S.C. § 1983 and 1985(3) claims of an HIV-positive prisoner administratively segregated from the general prison population.

Local 1812, American Fed'n of Gov't Employees v. United States. Sustaining State Department mandatory blood testing program on substantial governmental interest in determining individual fitness for duty.

Martinez v. School Board of Hillsborough County, Fla. Denying a preliminary injunction to enroll a child with AIDS to a trainable mentally handicapped (TMH) educational program.

McDuffie v. Rikers Island Medical Dep't. Dismissing 42 U.S.C. § claim of prisoner segregated from the general prison population because he was misdiagnosed as having AIDS.

McKee v. Miles Laboratories, Inc. Refusing to hold plasma manufacturers strictly liable for AIDS-related death caused by contaminated blood products.

Muhammad v. Frame. Dismissing 42 U.S.C. § claim of prisoner housed in the same cell block with prisoners diagnosed as having AIDS.

Ray v. The School Dist. of Desoto County. Granting preliminary injunction to allow children with AIDS to enroll i public school under § 540 of the Rehabilitation Act of 1973.

Thomas v. Atascadero Unified School Dist. Granting preliminary injunction to allow child with AIDS to enroll in public school under § 540 of the Rehabilitation Act of 1973.

United States v. Kazenbach. Dismissing on grounds of multiplicity two of three assault counts involving a prisoner with AIDS and three corrections officers.

United States v. Moore. Denying a motion for acquittal or new trial involving an AIDS-related assault charge.

Cases Decided in 1986

American Council of Life Ins. v. District of Columbia. Upholding ordinance prohibiting health, life, and disability insurers from discriminating against persons with AIDS or HIV infection.

Board of Educ. v. Cooperman. Reversing a commissioner of education order requiring school districts to admit children with AIDS pending an administrative hearing on the order.

Broadway Books v. Roberts. Sustaining an ordinance regulating adult theaters on substantial governmental interest in preventing the spread of AIDS.

City of N.Y. v. New Saint Mark's Baths. Granting a preliminary injunction to close bathhouses pursuant to state regulation aimed at preventing the spread of AIDS.

District 27 Community School Bd. v. Board of Educ. Holding that the Rehabilitation Act and the due process clause of the fourteenth amendment prevent the automatic exclusion of children with AIDS from attending public school in New York.

Doe v. Coughlin. Denying conjugal visit to prisoner with AIDS.

Feigly v. Jeffes. Dismissing for insufficient service of process prisoner's claim that prison food handlers should be screened for AIDS.

Fenton v. City of Philadelphia. Dismissing 42 U.S.C. § 1983 claim of prisoner who was accused by police of having AIDS.

First Penn-Pacific Life Ins. Co. v. Mock. Settling the estate of a possible victim of AIDS.

Flood v. Wyeth Laboratories. Distinguishing proposed legislative grant of immunity to developers of AIDS vaccine from denial of immunity to manufacturers of DPT vaccine.

Foy v. Owens. Dismissing prisoner's claim that potential carriers of AIDS should be quarantined from the general prison population.

In re Commitment of B.S. Authorizing the commitment of a mentally ill woman who coincidentally had AIDS.

Kentucky Cent. Life Ins. Co. v. Webster. Awarding monetary proceeds from life insurance policy to the estate of a person who died as a result of AIDS.

Klein v. Panic. Denying plaintiff's application for temporary restraining order in stock option suit of AIDS research company.

Powell v. Department of Corrections. Dismissing § 1983 claim of prisoner who tested positive for exposure to AIDS and was subsequently segregated from the general prison population.

Smith-Bey v. Captain of the Guard. Denying a motion to grant a preliminary injunction ordering prison officials to test each prisoner for AIDS with whom petitioner will be confined.

Shuttleworth v. Broward County. Holding that the Rehabilitation Act and the equal protection clause of the fourteenth amendment prevent discrimination against employees with AIDS.

Storms v. Department of Correctional Serv., State of N.Y. Dismissing due process claim of prison legal assistant representing prisoners with AIDS.

Torres v. City of Philadelphia Police Dep't Sex Crimes Unit. Dismissing for lack of specificity § 1983 claim that police officers intimidated arrestee by telling him he might have AIDS.

Williams v. Sumner. Dismissing constitutional claims of prisoner who was removed from work because he tested positive for AIDS.

Cases Decided in 1985

Albany County Dep't of Social Serv. *ex rel.* Sousis v. Seeberger. Rejecting claim that blood test in paternity suit would augment prison guard's susceptibility to AIDS.

Baker v. Wade. Denying motion to reopen trial involving constitutional attack on sodomy statute because of new evidence concerning AIDS.

Georgia *ex rel.* Slaton v. Fleck & Associates. Refusing removal to federal court of nuisance prosection of nightclub allegedly frequented by AIDS carriers.

Hyland Therapeutics v. Superior Ct. Refusing to hold plasma manufacturers strictly liable for AIDS-related death brought upon by contaminated blood product.

Menaldino *ex rel.* Smith v. Rawson. Rejecting claim that blood test in paternity suit would augment prison guard's susceptibility to AIDS.

New Jersey v. Muessig. Holding that prison system is equipped to handle AIDS.

Pawlisch v. Barry. Sustaining the removal of a board of health member who disagreed with county executive over AIDS policy.

South Fla. Blood Serv. v. Rasmussen. Rescinding on privacy grounds subpoena to blood bank by AIDS victim requesting names of blood donors.

Cases Decided Prior to 1985

Cordero v. Coughlin. Dismissing constitutional claims of prisoners with AIDS segregated from general prison population.

LaRocca v. Dahlsheim. Rejecting prisoner's challenge to prison policies concerning AIDS.